The Power of Grace Study Manual

Dr. Larry Ollison

Copyright 2025–Dr. Larry Ollison

All rights reserved. This book is protected by the copyright laws of the United States of America. This book may not be copied or reprinted for commercial gain or profit. The use of short quotations or occasional page copying for personal or group study is permitted and encouraged. Permission will be granted upon request. Unless otherwise indicated, all scripture quotations are taken from the *King James Version* of the Bible. Used by permission. All rights reserved.

All emphasis within Scripture quotations is the author's own. Please note that Harrison House's publishing style capitalizes certain pronouns in Scripture that refer to the Father, Son, and Holy Spirit, and may differ from some publishers' styles. Take note that the name satan and related names are not capitalized. We choose not to acknowledge him, even to the point of violating grammatical rules.

Harrison House P.O. Box 310, Shippensburg, PA 17257-0310

This book and all other Harrison House's books are available at Christian bookstores and distributors worldwide.

Reach us on the Internet: www.harrisonhouse.com.

ISBN 13 TP: 978-1-6675-1269-3

ISBN 13 eBook: 978-1-6675-1270-9

Contents

1. Rightly Dividing the Word ... 1
2. Spirit, Soul, and Body ... 9
3. Righteousness and Holiness Are Not the Same Thing ... 17
4. Grace and Faith — Partners in Salvation ... 25
5. Unskilled in the Word of Righteousness ... 33
6. Grace Does Not Come by Works ... 41
7. Grace Came Through Jesus Christ ... 49
8. Grace Is a Rest ... 57
9. Defining Moments ... 65
10. Your Destiny Depends on Grace ... 73
11. Grace Is Not a License to Sin ... 81
12. Grace Is Not Automatic ... 87
13. Growing in Grace ... 93
14. How to Obtain Grace ... 99
15. Your Words Affect the Power of Grace ... 105
16. Grace to Defeat the Works of the Flesh ... 113
17. Empowered by Grace ... 121

About the Publisher ... 129

Chapter 1

Rightly Dividing the Word

"Be diligent to present yourself approved to God, a worker who does not need to be ashamed, rightly dividing the word of truth." (2 Timothy 2:15, NKJV)

The day I purchased my first airplane remains one of the most thrilling moments of my life. My father, who served in the 8th Air Force during World War II, passed down to me a love for aviation—even though he worked on the ground in England. When my children went to college, I would sometimes fly their freshly laundered clothes to them. It probably would've been more cost-effective to buy them new clothes, but for a pilot, any excuse to fly is a good one. That passion came in handy one particular Sunday when I decided to fly out to hear a visiting friend from Australia speak at a church. The sky was clear, the autopilot was off, and I was simply enjoying the art of flying. But when it came time to land, the airport wasn't where it was supposed to be. I had been just a few degrees off the entire trip—what seemed like a small miscalculation had taken me far from my intended destination.

That day, I learned something critical: it doesn't matter how convinced you are that you're on the right path. If you're off—no matter how slightly—over time, you'll miss the mark completely. This principle applies with even greater weight when it comes to the Word of God. The Word itself is flawless, but our interpretation can be skewed. If we don't rightly divide it, we end up forming beliefs that take us further from truth, even if we start with good intentions. Like an inexperienced co-pilot focusing on one gauge while ignoring the rest, a believer who fixates on one verse without balancing it with the full counsel of Scripture is likely to crash doctrinally.

This is why the skill of rightly dividing the Word is essential. Just as a pilot must understand every instrument and how they work together, a believer must engage all aspects of biblical truth—grace, faith, holiness, righteousness, and beyond. One truth cannot cancel out another. For example, those who exalt grace while denouncing works often forget that James declared, "Faith without works is dead." (James 2:26) A balanced understanding of Scripture is like a puzzle coming together to reveal a complete picture of God's heart and plan.

So I ask you: Have you been flying your spiritual journey based on partial understanding? Are there areas of Scripture you've clung to without weighing them against the whole counsel of God? Your destination—and your ability to walk in truth—depends on whether or not you're rightly dividing the Word of Truth.

Focus Point

"Be diligent to present yourself approved to God, a worker who does not need to be ashamed, rightly dividing the word of truth." (2 Timothy 2:15, NKJV)

This verse is the anchor of this chapter because it places the responsibility of understanding Scripture squarely on the believer. It challenges us not only to read God's Word but to rightly divide it—to interpret it through the Spirit, with balance and precision. Just as a craftsman earns approval through skilled work, we are called to approach the Word with diligence and care, ensuring we do not mislead ourselves or others. This is the foundational call to spiritual maturity.

Main Theme

The main focus of this chapter is the urgency and necessity of rightly dividing the Word of God to avoid spiritual error and immaturity. The Word, though infallible, must be approached with understanding of foundational principles—such as spirit, soul, and body, the distinction between righteousness and holiness, and recognizing to whom each passage is addressed. When misapplied, even Scripture can be misused to foster confusion, false doctrines, and spiritual stagnation. The Word must be read in the light of revelation by the Holy Spirit and in the context of the entire Bible.

Rightly dividing the Word is not a suggestion; it is a safeguard for your soul.

Key Scriptures

- *"All Scripture is given by inspiration of God, and is profitable for doctrine, for reproof, for correction, for instruction in righteousness."* (2 Timothy 3:16, NKJV)
- *"For the word of God is living and powerful, and sharper than any two-edged sword, piercing even to the division of soul and spirit, and of joints and marrow, and is a discerner of the thoughts and intents of the heart."* (Hebrews 4:12, NKJV)
- *"My people are destroyed for lack of knowledge. Because you have rejected knowledge, I also will reject you from being priest for Me."* (Hosea 4:6, NKJV)

Key Points

- **Don't Rely on Assumptions** Believing you are right doesn't make you right. Even a minor deviation from truth can take you far off course.
- **Scripture Must Be Interpreted with Balance** Focusing on one principle while ignoring others can result in dangerous doctrinal imbalances.
- **Know to Whom the Scripture Is Written** All Scripture is for us, but not all Scripture is directed to us. Context is essential in interpretation.
- **The Spirit, Soul, and Body Must Be Understood** Without understanding our triune nature, confusion about sin, righteousness, and behavior will abound.
- **Faith and Works Are Not Opposed** Though salvation is by grace through faith, true faith produces works. One does not invalidate the other.
- **Error Often Stems from Isolated Truths** Even good doctrines, when removed from their biblical balance, can lead to serious theological error.
- **Right Division Requires Spiritual Maturity** The Word must be approached with study, diligence, and the guidance of the Holy Spirit—not with casual or carnal assumptions.

Journaling Questions

Journaling through this chapter helps lay a vital foundation for understanding how to read the Bible accurately and responsibly. The teaching is not merely theoretical—it is intensely practical and spiritual. By journaling, you open a space for the Holy Spirit to highlight personal biases, assumptions, or long-held misunderstandings. You begin to identify areas where deeper study is needed or where your spiritual GPS needs recalibration.

As you reflect, the Holy Spirit will begin to show you specific Scriptures you've misunderstood or overlooked. Journaling these revelations allows transformation to take root. This process isn't just about gaining knowledge—it's about yielding to the Spirit, who rightly divides truth within you so you can walk in the fullness of grace and maturity.

Examining Your Course

Have I ever realized I was "a few degrees off" in my understanding of God's Word? What was the outcome?

_____
_____
_____
_____
_____
_____
_____

Scripture in Context

Have I taken verses out of context without knowing who they were originally written to or why?

_____
_____
_____
_____
_____
_____

Spiritual Navigation

Do I know the difference between my spirit, soul, and body—and how they influence how I receive the Word?

_____
_____
_____
_____
_____
_____
_____

The Danger of Overemphasis

Have I ever emphasized one biblical truth at the expense of others? How did it impact my faith walk?

_____
_____
_____
_____
_____
_____
_____

Building with Balance

In what areas of my spiritual life do I need to step back and ensure I'm seeing the whole picture of God's truth?

_____
_____
_____
_____
_____
_____
_____

Actionable Steps

Recognize the Need for Adjustment
Just as a pilot corrects course when veering off, begin to ask the Holy Spirit to show you any area of misalignment in your theology or interpretation of Scripture.

Anchor Your Study in the Full Counsel of Scripture
Make a commitment to study at least one cross-reference for every verse you read during devotional time this week. This will train your spiritual sight to zoom out and consider broader context.

Invite the Holy Spirit as Your Instructor
Before reading the Bible, take time each day to specifically invite the Holy Spirit to teach, guide, and reveal. Scripture is not just intellectual—it is spiritual. Let Him be your compass.

Personal Reflection

As you meditate on this chapter, allow the truth of rightly dividing the Word to examine your spiritual patterns. Have you allowed assumptions or limited knowledge to lead your journey? Ask yourself: where am I depending more on tradition or emotion than on the rightly interpreted truth of God's Word? This is not a rebuke—it's an invitation to adjust and move into deeper clarity and maturity.

Embracing this responsibility is not a burden; it's a privilege. God wants to partner with you in your spiritual growth. Through daily study, reflection, and submission to the Holy Spirit, you will begin to discern the difference between man's interpretation and divine revelation. Let this be the start of a new chapter in how you encounter God's Word.

What parts of my understanding have been based on assumption? What truths have I ignored because they were uncomfortable? Am I ready to make the shift to rightly divide God's Word—no matter the cost?

_____
_____
_____
_____
_____

Closing Prayer: *Lord, I desire to know You through Your Word. Teach me how to rightly divide truth—not according to my feelings or traditions, but by Your Spirit. I surrender my mind and assumptions to You. Train me like a skilled worker to interpret Your Word faithfully. Thank You for Your patience as I grow in maturity. In Jesus' name, amen.*

Chapter 2

Spirit, Soul, and Body

"Now may the God of peace Himself sanctify you completely; and may your whole spirit, soul, and body be preserved blameless at the coming of our Lord Jesus Christ." (1 Thessalonians 5:23, NKJV)

It was not until I deeply studied the Word of God that I realized the importance of knowing how we are made—spirit, soul, and body. Understanding this truth opened my eyes to why some Scriptures seemed to contradict others and why believers often struggle with guilt, confusion, or condemnation after salvation. It became clear to me that much of the spiritual frustration believers experience comes from misunderstanding who they really are in Christ and how the parts of their being interact with one another. I came to see that if we confuse what part of us is born again with what part still needs renewal, we will constantly doubt our righteousness and question our salvation.

Most Christians assume their soul and spirit are the same, but they are not. Your spirit is the real you—the part that is reborn when you accept Christ. Your soul is your mind, will, emotions, and intellect, and your body is simply your physical house. When you are saved, your spirit becomes new, perfect, and sinless. But your soul must be renewed daily with the Word of God, and your body remains unchanged until the resurrection. Failing to understand these distinctions leads to confusion, false doctrine, and often, unnecessary shame.

This revelation also explains why born-again believers still sin. It's not the spirit that sins; it's the soul and the body acting in rebellion or ignorance. When Scripture says "he who is born of God does not sin," it is speaking of the spirit man—the part of us that is born of incorruptible seed. But when Scripture says "if we say we have no sin, we deceive ourselves," it is speaking of our soul and body. These aren't contradictions—they're clarifications that come when we rightly divide the Word and understand our makeup.

Have you ever wondered why you still struggle with certain behaviors or thoughts even after salvation? It's because your soul and body are still catching up to the reality of what has already happened in your spirit. But once you grasp this truth, you will walk with freedom, confidence, and clarity in your relationship with God.

Focus Point

"Now may the God of peace Himself sanctify you completely; and may your whole spirit, soul, and body be preserved blameless at the coming of our Lord Jesus Christ." (1 Thessalonians 5:23, NKJV)

This verse is vital because it reveals that we are a three-part being, each part with a specific function. It reinforces that sanctification—becoming like Christ—is a complete work affecting our spirit (instantly made new), our soul (progressively renewed), and our body (eventually glorified). Without this framework, believers will misapply Scripture and live under confusion and defeat. God wants to preserve every part of us blameless—not just our actions, but our nature, our thoughts, and even our physical body when Jesus returns.

Main Theme

The central message of this chapter is the biblical revelation of man as a triune being: spirit, soul, and body, and the essential need to distinguish how each part functions in salvation and sanctification. Your spirit is instantly made righteous when you're born again. Your soul must be renewed daily through the Word of God and obedience. Your body remains fleshly until glorified. Without understanding this truth, it is impossible to walk in confidence or experience true victory in your Christian life.

You are not a body trying to be spiritual—you are a spirit learning to govern your soul and body through truth.

Key Scriptures

- *"Therefore, if anyone is in Christ, he is a new creation; old things have passed away; behold, all things have become new."* (2 Corinthians 5:17, NKJV)
- *"Whoever has been born of God does not sin, for His seed remains in him; and he cannot sin, because he has been born of God."* (1 John 3:9, NKJV)
- *"And do not be conformed to this world, but be transformed by the renewing of your mind, that you may prove what is that good and acceptable and perfect will of God."* (Romans 12:2, NKJV)

Key Points

- **You Are a Three-Part Being** You are spirit, soul, and body. Understanding this truth is the foundation of spiritual maturity and biblical interpretation.
- **Your Spirit Is Instantly Made New** At salvation, your spirit becomes a new creation, filled with the Spirit of God and incapable of sin. It is sealed and secure.
- **Your Soul Must Be Renewed** The soul—your mind, will, emotions—must be trained daily by the Word. Without renewal, it can resist the spirit's leadership.
- **Your Body Is Not Saved Yet** Your body remains fleshly and subject to sin. It must be disciplined and brought under the control of the spirit.
- **The Heart Is Not the Spirit** The heart is the overflow reservoir of your inner life. It is influenced by both soul and spirit and reveals itself through speech.
- **Renewing the Mind Unlocks Victory** As your mind aligns with the Word, your soul and body come under the authority of the spirit, resulting in transformation.
- **God Will One Day Redeem Your Body** When Christ returns, your physical body will be glorified to match the sinless nature of your spirit. This is the completion of salvation.

Journaling Questions

Journaling through this chapter invites deep reflection on the inner life and identity of a believer. By clarifying the differences between spirit, soul, and body, this teaching dismantles spiritual confusion and empowers believers to grow in sanctification with confidence. Journaling allows you to examine what part of your being has been ruling your decisions and where your mind needs renewal.

When you respond to these questions with honesty, you'll begin to receive clarity on areas that have felt contradictory or frustrating. You'll start to realize that your struggle is not about your salvation but about soul management. As you write, the Holy Spirit will help you distinguish truth from lies, freedom from bondage, and Spirit-led living from flesh-led chaos.

Distinguishing the Real You

Am I living from my spirit, or am I being ruled by my soul and body? How can I shift that starting today?

_____
_____
_____
_____
_____
_____
_____

Understanding the Born-Again Nature

Do I believe that my spirit is truly righteous and sinless? Or have I been mixing up my soul's struggle with my spiritual identity?

_____
_____
_____
_____
_____
_____

Mind Renewal Habits

Am I actively renewing my mind with the Word of God? What areas of my thinking need alignment with Scripture?

_____
_____
_____
_____
_____
_____

Heart Inventory

What has been filling my heart lately—faith-filled truth or polluted thoughts from the world? What needs to be removed?

_____
_____
_____
_____
_____
_____

Disciplining the Body

In what areas has my body led my decisions instead of my spirit? What steps do I need to take to bring my flesh under control?

_____
_____
_____
_____
_____
_____

Actionable Steps

Feed Your Spirit Daily
You grow what you feed. Begin every day this week with a spiritual meal—reading and confessing the Word to feed your spirit, not just your soul.

Renew Your Mind Intentionally
Write down one Scripture each day and meditate on it. Speak it aloud multiple times and observe how your emotions and decisions shift.

Discipline Your Body with Purpose
Choose one habit where your body has been in control (overeating, sloth, addiction) and start a fast or discipline plan to regain spiritual authority.

Personal Reflection

Understanding that you are a spirit with a soul living in a body will transform the way you walk with God. You no longer have to live under the weight of guilt or confusion when you miss the mark. Instead, you can begin to see where the correction is needed—in your mind or behavior—but not in your spirit, which has been made perfect by Christ. This frees you to mature without shame and grow with purpose.

The Holy Spirit, who dwells in your born-again spirit, is committed to guiding your soul and disciplining your body. But He waits for your cooperation. You are not alone, and you are not powerless. As you continue to grow in understanding and yield to His work, you will see increasing victory in every area of your life. This journey is not about perfection—it's about daily surrender and obedience.

Am I willing to take ownership of renewing my mind? Will I stop blaming my spirit for what my soul or body is doing? Am I ready to live from the inside out—with the spirit leading the way?

_____
_____
_____
_____
_____

Closing Prayer: *Lord, thank You for making me a new creation. I am a spirit, I have a soul, and I live in a body. Teach me how to walk with this understanding daily. Help me renew my mind with Your Word and bring my body into obedience. I declare that my spirit is righteous, and I choose to live from that truth. In Jesus' name, amen.*

Chapter 3

Righteousness and Holiness Are Not the Same Thing

"Pursue peace with all people, and holiness, without which no one will see the Lord." (Hebrews 12:14, NKJV)

For years I listened to believers use the words "righteousness" and "holiness" as if they were interchangeable. But the more I studied the Word, the more I saw a striking difference—one that had immense spiritual consequences if misunderstood. The confusion surrounding these terms has left many believers trapped in a cycle of performance, guilt, or self-righteousness. I knew firsthand what it was like to strive for God's approval through behavior rather than receiving it through grace. But when I understood that righteousness is a gift, and holiness is a choice, it revolutionized the way I walked with God.

The moment we are born again, we are made righteous by the finished work of Jesus Christ. Nothing we do, no matter how good, can earn righteousness. But holiness—ah, that's different. Holiness is not imputed; it's pursued. It is our obedient response to the righteousness we've already received. When this truth clicked for me, it was as though the fog lifted. The Word came alive in new ways, and Scriptures that once seemed contradictory now aligned in perfect harmony. Suddenly, I wasn't trying to become righteous—I already was. I just needed to let my lifestyle reflect it through holiness.

The distinction is vital. If you confuse righteousness with holiness, you will start believing your behavior determines your right standing with God. You'll judge others harshly and yourself even more severely. But if you understand that righteousness is a position granted by grace, and holiness is the lifestyle response to that grace, then you'll walk in both confidence and conviction. Grace will no longer be a license to sin but an empowerment to live holy.

So here's the question: Have you been trying to earn what God has already given? Or have you neglected the call to holiness because you misunderstood grace? It's time to separate these truths and let each do its work in your life.

Focus Point

"Pursue peace with all people, and holiness, without which no one will see the Lord." (Hebrews 12:14, NKJV)

This verse underscores the gravity of holiness. It is not optional. While righteousness is a gift given through faith in Christ, holiness is a call to action—to live a life that reflects the God who now dwells in you. Without it, we cannot walk in the fullness of God's presence. Holiness doesn't produce salvation, but it does demonstrate transformation. It is the visible fruit of an invisible root—your righteous standing in Christ.

Main Theme

The primary message of this chapter is this: Righteousness and holiness are not the same, and confusing the two leads to spiritual immaturity and religious bondage. Righteousness is a gift of position received at salvation; holiness is a lifestyle of obedience cultivated daily. Both are essential, but they operate differently. Understanding this distinction brings freedom from works-based striving and empowers you to live out the reality of grace with purity, integrity, and boldness.

You are made righteous by grace; you become holy by choice.

Key Scriptures

- *"For He made Him who knew no sin to be sin for us, that we might become the righteousness of God in Him."* (2 Corinthians 5:21, NKJV)
- *"I beseech you therefore, brethren, by the mercies of God, that you present your bodies a living sacrifice, holy, acceptable to God, which is your reasonable service."* (Romans 12:1, NKJV)

- *"Therefore gird up the loins of your mind, be sober, and rest your hope fully upon the grace that is to be brought to you at the revelation of Jesus Christ... but as He who called you is holy, you also be holy in all your conduct."* (1 Peter 1:13, 15, NKJV)

Key Points

- **Righteousness Is a Gift** You cannot earn righteousness; it is freely given when you receive Christ by faith. It is your position before God.
- **Holiness Is a Lifestyle** Holiness is not a gift; it's a decision. It is the practical expression of your obedience and devotion to God.
- **Confusing the Two Breeds Legalism** When righteousness and holiness are blurred, people strive to earn what is already theirs, resulting in spiritual frustration.
- **Grace Empowers Holiness** Grace doesn't nullify the call to holiness—it enables it. Grace provides the strength to walk uprightly.
- **Righteousness Is Instant, Holiness Is Progressive** The moment you are born again, you are made righteous. Holiness, however, is a process that unfolds as you submit to God's Word.
- **Righteousness Qualifies You, Holiness Sets You Apart** Righteousness gives you access to the Father. Holiness makes you useful for His purposes and reflects His character.
- **Both Are Essential for Maturity** You cannot grow spiritually without both. Righteousness establishes identity; holiness shapes integrity.

Journaling Questions

This chapter is foundational for anyone struggling with legalism, guilt, or the burden of performance. Journaling through this topic creates space for the Holy Spirit to expose lies you've believed about your standing with God. It also helps you confront the areas in your life where holiness has been optional or neglected.

As you write, you'll begin to recognize patterns—areas where you've unknowingly tried to earn God's approval or where you've excused sin under the guise of grace. Journaling opens your eyes to the power of righteousness and the necessity of holiness, setting you on a path of spiritual balance and maturity.

Understanding Your Position

Do I truly believe I am righteous in Christ right now—not because of what I do, but because of what Jesus did?

_____
_____
_____
_____
_____
_____
_____

Evaluating My Pursuit of Holiness

Am I daily choosing to walk in holiness, or have I become complacent in areas that displease God?

_____
_____
_____
_____
_____
_____

Uncovering Legalism

Have I ever measured my righteousness by my behavior? In what ways has this mindset affected my relationship with God?

_____
_____
_____

Grace Misunderstood

Have I misunderstood grace as permission to remain unchanged, rather than empowerment to live transformed?

_____
_____
_____
_____
_____
_____
_____

Living in Balance

How can I honor both the gift of righteousness and the pursuit of holiness in my daily life?

_____
_____
_____
_____
_____
_____
_____

Actionable Steps

Acknowledge Your Righteous Standing
Each morning, begin by declaring aloud: "I am the righteousness of God in Christ." Let this truth shape your identity.

Pursue Holiness Intentionally
Choose one area of your life—speech, entertainment, relationships—where you will consciously pursue holiness this week.

Separate Position from Performance
When you fall short, remind yourself: "My righteousness is in Christ. I choose now to walk in holiness by His grace." Don't let failure define your position.

Personal Reflection

You've just encountered a truth that could dismantle years of religious striving or spiritual apathy. Righteousness is not your reward—it is your starting point. Holiness is not your burden—it is your calling. When you stop confusing the two, your Christian walk becomes joyful, fruitful, and grounded in grace. God is not asking for perfection to earn His approval. He's asking for surrender because you already have it.

This chapter calls you to both confidence and responsibility. Confidence that you are secure in your salvation. Responsibility to reflect that salvation in how you live. These two truths—righteousness and holiness—are not at war. They are allies, working together to form the image of Christ in you. When grace teaches you who you are, holiness becomes your joyful response.

Do I walk daily with the confidence of righteousness? Am I responding to grace with a lifestyle of holiness? What would my life look like if both truths were fully embraced?

Closing Prayer: *Father, thank You for making me righteous through Jesus Christ. I did nothing to earn it, yet You gave it freely. Teach me now to walk in holiness—not to gain Your approval, but to reflect Your nature. Help me surrender daily to Your Word and Spirit. Let righteousness anchor me and holiness shape me. In Jesus' name, amen.*

Chapter 4

Grace and Faith — Partners in Salvation

"For by grace you have been saved through faith, and that not of yourselves; it is the gift of God, not of works, lest anyone should boast." (Ephesians 2:8-9, NKJV)

There was a time when I wrestled with the question: If grace is God's unmerited favor and faith is our response, how do they work together? I had heard teachings that emphasized one over the other—some that glorified faith to the point of striving, others that elevated grace to the point of passivity. I've even heard someone say, "It's all grace! Faith isn't necessary!" But when I dug into Scripture, I realized the error in those extremes. Grace and faith are not enemies. They are not even separate lanes. They are partners—co-laborers in the work of salvation. One without the other is powerless. Together, they unlock the full measure of God's redemptive plan.

This revelation came alive for me when I began to see how Scripture interweaves the two. Grace is God reaching down. Faith is man reaching up. Grace provides. Faith receives. The two are inseparable in the life of the believer. You are saved by grace—but only through faith. That means salvation wasn't just dumped on you against your will. It required a response. God made the way through Jesus Christ, and your faith in that sacrifice activated grace in your life. That's not works—it's participation. It's not earning—it's believing.

The same is true for every other area of the Christian life. Healing, provision, righteousness, and peace are all accessed by grace through faith. When believers misunderstand this, they either slip into legalism—trying to earn what God has already given—or spiritual laziness—waiting for God to do everything with no engagement from their end. The truth is balanced.

Grace is God's part. Faith is ours. We don't work to earn grace, but we must believe to receive it.

So here's the challenge: Are you fully walking in the partnership of grace and faith? Or have you emphasized one while neglecting the other? If grace has been extended, then the invitation is open. But faith is the hand that reaches out to take hold of what God has freely provided.

Focus Point

"For by grace you have been saved through faith, and that not of yourselves; it is the gift of God, not of works, lest anyone should boast." (Ephesians 2:8-9, NKJV)

This verse is one of the clearest and most powerful declarations of the partnership between grace and faith. It reveals that salvation is not a product of human effort or religious duty. Instead, it is the result of God's grace, activated and made personal through our faith. The verse also shuts the door to pride by confirming that even faith is not something we conjure up on our own—it is a response to God's initiative.

Main Theme

The main focus of this chapter is the divine partnership between grace and faith in the work of salvation. Grace is the unearned, undeserved favor of God that made salvation possible through Jesus Christ. Faith is the hand that reaches out to receive that gift. They do not compete with one another—they complete one another. Without grace, there would be nothing to believe for. Without faith, grace remains unreceived. Every benefit of the New Covenant is accessed this way: by grace, through faith.

Grace provides. Faith receives. Together, they unlock salvation's full reward.

Key Scriptures

- *"Therefore it is of faith that it might be according to grace, so that the promise might be sure to all the seed..."* (Romans 4:16, NKJV)

- *"And if by grace, then it is no longer of works; otherwise grace is no longer grace."* (Romans 11:6, NKJV)
- *"We have access by faith into this grace in which we stand, and rejoice in hope of the glory of God."* (Romans 5:2, NKJV)

Key Points

- **Grace and Faith Are a Divine Partnership** Salvation is not grace alone or faith alone—it is the union of both. Grace gives; faith takes.
- **Grace Is God's Part** Grace is the power of God extended toward you. It is unearned and cannot be worked for.
- **Faith Is Your Part** Faith is the personal response to grace. It is not a work—it's a yielding, a trust, a believing that activates what God has done.
- **You Cannot Earn Grace** Any attempt to earn salvation nullifies grace. Works-based righteousness cancels the free gift God intended.
- **Faith Does Not Replace Grace** Faith doesn't add to grace or replace it. It simply accepts and agrees with what grace has already done.
- **Everything from God Comes This Way** Not just salvation—healing, provision, peace, and strength all come by grace, through faith.
- **Grace Is Not Passive** Though freely given, grace still requires action—faith must be exercised to experience the fullness of what God has provided.

Journaling Questions

Journaling through this chapter helps expose any imbalance in your understanding of grace and faith. Many believers unknowingly swing toward one side or the other, either becoming exhausted trying to earn God's blessings, or passive in waiting for Him to do everything without their engagement. Reflection on these truths allows you to find that divine balance, where you can rest in grace while actively responding in faith.

When you write through these concepts, you'll begin to discern where you've operated in self-effort, or perhaps where you've failed to activate faith at all. Journaling provides the Holy Spirit room to highlight areas where your understanding of this divine partnership can grow stronger, freeing you from both legalism and lethargy.

Grace or Works?

Have I been trying to earn what God has already given by grace? In what areas of my walk with God am I striving instead of believing?

_____
_____
_____
_____
_____
_____
_____

Responding in Faith

Am I actively responding to God's promises with faith, or am I waiting passively for something to happen?

_____
_____
_____
_____
_____
_____

Faith for the Present

Where do I need to apply faith right now—in a relationship, my finances, my health, or my calling?

_____
_____
_____
_____
_____
_____

Misunderstanding Grace

Have I misunderstood grace as something that requires no response from me? How can I begin to respond differently?

_____
_____
_____
_____
_____
_____
_____

Faith as a Lifestyle

How can I develop a lifestyle of faith that continually receives from the storehouse of God's grace?

_____
_____
_____
_____
_____
_____
_____

Actionable Steps

Identify Where You're Striving
Examine an area of your life where you've been trying to earn God's favor. Stop striving and begin confessing the grace that's already yours.

Activate Faith Through the Word
Find a Scripture that speaks to your current need. Speak it aloud each day this week and thank God that grace has already provided it.

Stop Waiting—Start Receiving
Don't delay obedience waiting for more signs or feelings. If grace has made it available, step out in faith today. Take a small action that reflects trust in God.

Personal Reflection

The harmony between grace and faith is the heartbeat of the Christian life. Grace is the outstretched hand of the Father—offering everything you need. Faith is your reaching hand that says, "Yes, I believe." You don't have to live in fear of not doing enough, nor should you live in apathy assuming God will do everything without you. You are invited into a partnership —a daily walk where grace supplies and faith applies.

Let this truth liberate you. No longer live as if God is withholding from you. He has already given. And no longer live as if faith is merely intellectual agreement. It is bold, responsive action to the promises of God. When you live in this balance, you'll find rest and power working together in every area of your life.

Have I fully embraced God's grace in my life? Am I responding with faith, or just hoping things change? What is one promise from God that I need to receive today—by grace, through faith?

Closing Prayer: *Father, thank You for Your grace that made salvation, healing, and every blessing available. I know I cannot earn it, and I do not want to try. Teach me to respond in faith —to believe, to receive, and to walk in what You've already done. Let grace and faith work together in my life as You intended. In Jesus' name, amen.*

Chapter 5

Unskilled in the Word of Righteousness

"But solid food belongs to those who are of full age, that is, those who by reason of use have their senses exercised to discern both good and evil." (Hebrews 5:14, NKJV)

I remember sitting with a group of believers many years ago when a well-meaning friend made a comment that left the room quiet. He said, "I know I'm just a sinner saved by grace—I'll never really be righteous until I get to heaven." The sad part was, everyone nodded in agreement. But something inside me stirred. I had already begun to discover a powerful truth in Scripture: We are not just sinners saved by grace—we have been made the righteousness of God in Christ. And those who continue to speak otherwise, though sincere, are unskilled in the Word of righteousness.

This is a topic the writer of Hebrews addresses directly. Many Christians remain spiritual infants because they cannot grasp or handle the meat of righteousness. They still stumble over the idea that they have already been made right with God—not through works, but through the finished work of Christ. Because of this, they remain stuck in cycles of guilt, condemnation, and powerlessness. Without understanding righteousness, you cannot operate in boldness. You will always feel disqualified.

But righteousness isn't something you grow into. It's not something you earn through good behavior. It is a gift—imparted at salvation—and your spiritual maturity is directly tied to how skilled you become in that truth. The more you exercise and apply your understanding of righteousness, the more authority you will walk in. It's not arrogance—it's confidence in what Jesus accomplished.

So, I ask: Are you living like a forgiven sinner, always hoping to be worthy someday? Or are you growing skilled in the Word of righteousness, knowing that you are who God says you are—right now?

Focus Point

"But solid food belongs to those who are of full age, that is, those who by reason of use have their senses exercised to discern both good and evil." (Hebrews 5:14, NKJV)

This verse reveals that spiritual maturity doesn't come from simply hearing truth—it comes from practicing it. The Word of righteousness is not just head knowledge; it's a lived experience. Those who use it—who apply it—develop spiritual discernment and strength. They move from milk to meat. This passage challenges us to grow up, not by trying harder, but by believing deeper in what Christ has done.

Main Theme

The heart of this chapter is a call to spiritual maturity through becoming skilled in the truth of righteousness. Many believers remain immature because they don't know who they are in Christ. They still see themselves as unworthy, sinful, or disqualified. But the New Covenant declares that righteousness has been imparted to the believer at salvation. To be "skilled in the Word of righteousness" means to understand, confess, and live in the reality of being right with God now—not someday in the future. This knowledge separates spiritual infants from mature sons and daughters.

Spiritual growth begins when you stop trying to become righteous and start living from the righteousness you already have.

Key Scriptures

- *"For he who lacks these things is shortsighted, even to blindness, and has forgotten that he was cleansed from his old sins."* (2 Peter 1:9, NKJV)
- *"For He made Him who knew no sin to be sin for us, that we might become the righteousness of God in Him."* (2 Corinthians 5:21, NKJV)

- *"I do not set aside the grace of God; for if righteousness comes through the law, then Christ died in vain."* (Galatians 2:21, NKJV)

Key Points

- **Righteousness Is a Present Reality** You are not becoming righteous—you were made righteous the moment you were born again.
- **Immaturity Denies Identity** Those who say "I'm just a sinner" after salvation are unskilled in the Word of righteousness. They haven't matured in identity.
- **Practice Produces Discernment** Spiritual strength comes not just from hearing truth, but from using it—walking in it daily.
- **Righteousness Isn't Earned** Trying to earn right standing with God is a rejection of grace and an insult to the cross.
- **Mature Believers Walk in Confidence** Understanding righteousness produces boldness in prayer, authority in action, and peace in identity.
- **Guilt Reveals Immaturity** Ongoing guilt over past sins reveals a lack of understanding of the cleansing power of righteousness.
- **You Must Renew Your Mind Daily** To walk in righteousness, you must renew your thinking with the truth of who you are in Christ.

Journaling Questions

Journaling through this chapter invites you to confront one of the most foundational truths of your Christian life—your identity in Christ. This is not about feelings or performance. It's about whether you are fully convinced of what God says is already true about you. As you reflect, the Holy Spirit will begin revealing areas where you've lived more from guilt than from grace.

This process helps expose the subtle lies you've believed: that you need to work harder for God's approval, that you're never quite enough, that righteousness is some distant goal. Journaling gives you space to reject those lies and embrace your true identity. The more you do, the more mature, confident, and spiritually effective you'll become.

Your View of Righteousness

Do I truly believe I am righteous in Christ right now, or do I still see righteousness as something I have to achieve?

_____
_____
_____
_____
_____
_____
_____
_____

Dealing with Guilt

Am I still carrying guilt for sins that have already been forgiven? What does that reveal about my understanding of righteousness?

_____
_____
_____
_____
_____
_____

Signs of Maturity

What are some ways I can begin to practice and walk in the Word of righteousness daily?

_____
_____
_____
_____
_____
_____

Unlearning Religion

Have I been living under religious pressure to earn God's love? What truth from this chapter breaks that off?

_____
_____
_____
_____
_____
_____

Confidence in Christ

How would my prayer life, relationships, or decisions change if I walked in full confidence of my righteous identity?

_____
_____
_____
_____
_____
_____

Actionable Steps

Confess Your Identity Daily
Each morning, declare aloud: "I am the righteousness of God in Christ. I am clean, accepted, and empowered." Let that truth shape your day.

Identify and Replace Lies
Write down one religious lie you've believed about earning righteousness. Then replace it with Scripture and truth. Speak it often.

Walk in Confidence Today

Choose one situation—at work, at home, or in prayer—where you will step into boldness, knowing that you are right with God.

Personal Reflection

This chapter is a wake-up call to grow up spiritually—not through striving, but through believing. You are not righteous because you act right. You act right because you are righteous. When you embrace this truth, your Christian life stops being a struggle and starts becoming a joy. You stop trying to impress God and start partnering with Him.

Don't let immaturity rob you of confidence. You've been made new. Righteousness is not a goal—it's your foundation. The more you build on it, the stronger you become. Your authority, your boldness, your peace—they all flow from this place of secure identity.

Am I still living like a sinner, or am I standing in my righteousness? What spiritual maturity am I missing because I've misunderstood my identity? Am I ready to become skilled in the Word of righteousness—starting today?

Closing Prayer: *Father, thank You for making me righteous through Christ. I repent for every time I've tried to earn what You already gave. Help me grow skilled in this truth—not just hearing it, but practicing it. Let confidence, boldness, and peace rise up in me as I live from my new identity. In Jesus' name, amen.*

Chapter 6

Grace Does Not Come by Works

"And if by grace, then it is no longer of works; otherwise grace is no longer grace. But if it is of works, it is no longer grace; otherwise work is no longer work." (Romans 11:6, NKJV)

I remember a time early in my ministry when I was praying fervently—maybe even desperately—for God's favor on a certain situation. I found myself trying to convince Him through my good behavior, my recent victories, and even the hours I had spent studying and praying. In that moment, I thought I was practicing faith. But I was really attempting to trade my works for God's grace. That moment marked a turning point in my understanding of how the grace of God actually operates.

You see, grace does not come by works. It never has, and it never will. Grace is unearned. It is undeserved. It is unpurchasable. The moment you try to earn it, you forfeit it. It's like trying to pay for a gift that's already been paid in full by someone else—it dishonors the giver and undermines the gift. Yet, many believers unknowingly fall into the trap of trying to "qualify" for grace through religious activity, hoping their performance will impress God. But grace cannot be earned. If it could, it wouldn't be grace.

The Apostle Paul addressed this repeatedly in his letters to the early Church. The Galatians, for example, started in grace but quickly drifted back into works, trying to achieve by law what they had begun in the Spirit. Paul warned them that if they tried to be justified by the law, they had fallen from grace—not in the sense of losing salvation, but in walking away from the power of unearned favor. Grace is either all God or not at all.

So I ask you: Are you trying to earn what can only be received? Are you praying, reading, giving, and serving from a place of sonship—or are you still striving to prove yourself? The answer to that question will determine whether you're operating in works or walking in grace.

Focus Point

"And if by grace, then it is no longer of works; otherwise grace is no longer grace." (Romans 11:6, NKJV)

This verse draws a hard line between grace and works. It doesn't allow for mixture. Grace cannot be partially earned. If something must be worked for, it is a wage—not grace. Paul's words make it unmistakably clear: once you try to earn grace, it ceases to be grace altogether. This verse dismantles performance-based Christianity and refocuses us on the gift of God.

Main Theme

The central truth of this chapter is that grace is a gift that cannot be earned by works. When you attempt to work for grace—whether consciously or unconsciously—you actually remove yourself from the flow of grace. The temptation to earn God's love, favor, or acceptance through religious activity is strong, but it leads to frustration, burnout, and pride. True transformation happens not when you labor to receive grace, but when you rest in the grace already given.

Grace cannot be earned. It can only be believed and received.

Key Scriptures

- *"You have become estranged from Christ, you who attempt to be justified by law; you have fallen from grace."* (Galatians 5:4, NKJV)
- *"But God, who is rich in mercy, because of His great love with which He loved us… made us alive together with Christ (by grace you have been saved)."* (Ephesians 2:4–5, NKJV)
- *"I do not set aside the grace of God; for if righteousness comes through the law, then Christ died in vain."* (Galatians 2:21, NKJV)

Key Points

- **Grace and Works Cannot Mix** The moment you attempt to earn grace, it stops being grace and becomes a transaction.
- **Falling from Grace Means Returning to Works** To fall from grace isn't about losing salvation—it's about abandoning faith for law-based righteousness.
- **Grace Is a Gift from Start to Finish** You are saved by grace, you grow by grace, and you are sustained by grace—not by your performance.
- **Religious Activity Can Be Deceptive** Reading your Bible, praying, or giving are good—but they don't earn grace. They're responses to grace, not requirements for it.
- **Pride Is the Root of Earning** The human desire to earn favor from God stems from pride. Grace, by nature, requires humility to receive.
- **Resting in Grace Produces Fruit** Ironically, the less you strive to earn grace, the more fruitful your life becomes because you're operating by the Spirit.
- **Grace Keeps You Focused on Christ** Trying to earn God's love puts your focus on yourself. Receiving grace keeps your focus on Jesus.

Journaling Questions

Journaling through this chapter invites you to confront the subtle ways you've tried to earn what God already gave freely. Performance-based Christianity can hide behind spiritual language and good intentions. But at its root, it's bondage. It's exhausting. Grace invites you into rest, not resignation—but rest rooted in trust that God has already done the work through Christ.

As you journal, you'll likely discover habits, motivations, or beliefs that were birthed from insecurity or fear rather than grace. Let the Holy Spirit show you where striving still exists. Then allow the truth of God's gift to settle the matter once and for all: you are already loved. You are already accepted. You are already enough in Christ.

Works Mentality

Have I been trying to earn God's favor or grace through my actions or spiritual disciplines?

_____
_____
_____
_____
_____
_____
_____

Motivation Check

Am I doing good things—like prayer, giving, or serving—because I love God, or because I'm trying to feel worthy?

_____
_____
_____
_____
_____
_____

Recognizing the Trap

Have I ever felt that if I didn't "do enough," God would be disappointed in me? Where did that belief originate?

_____
_____
_____
_____
_____

Receiving Freely

What would it look like to fully receive grace with no strings attached? How would that change my thoughts or actions?

_____
_____
_____
_____
_____
_____

Living in Gratitude

How can I turn my works from effort into expressions of love and gratitude for the grace I've already received?

_____
_____
_____
_____
_____
_____

Actionable Steps

Identify the Area of Striving
Ask the Holy Spirit to show you where you're still trying to earn grace. Write it down. Then surrender it through prayer and confession.

Shift Your Language
Stop saying things like "I have to earn," "I need to deserve," or "God will love me if…" Replace them with "God has already given," "Jesus is enough," and "I receive by faith."

Rest, Don't Retreat

Take one day this week to intentionally rest in grace. Not to avoid your responsibilities, but to celebrate the finished work of Christ. Use that day to thank Him—not to prove anything, but to enjoy everything.

Personal Reflection

Grace is the great equalizer. It leaves no room for boasting and no place for striving. When you truly receive it, it doesn't make you lazy—it makes you worship. You don't read the Bible to earn God's favor; you read because He already favors you. You don't give or serve to prove yourself; you do it because you are already accepted. That shift changes everything.

There's freedom in knowing you can stop performing for love that's already yours. There's power in laying down works-based righteousness and picking up the righteousness of Christ. Grace frees you to live boldly, joyfully, and effectively. But first, it requires surrender—the kind of surrender that stops trying to earn and simply begins to receive.

Have I confused grace with reward? Am I still trying to earn something Jesus already purchased? Am I willing to lay down my works and receive the free gift of grace today—with no conditions?

Closing Prayer: *Father, thank You for the grace that I could never earn. Forgive me for trying to perform for what You've already provided through Jesus. I surrender my striving and receive Your love, Your favor, and Your presence as a gift. Teach me to live from grace—not for it. In Jesus' name, amen.*

Chapter 7

Grace Came Through Jesus Christ

"For the law was given through Moses, but grace and truth came through Jesus Christ." (John 1:17, NKJV)

I remember years ago reading the Old Testament and feeling overwhelmed by the long list of commands, rituals, and sacrifices. The law was exacting and exhaustive. It left no room for error and no path for true relationship. Yet, the New Testament introduced something different—Someone different. Jesus didn't come to extend the law; He came to fulfill it. He didn't come with condemnation, but with compassion. With Him came the arrival of something new: grace and truth. And this grace didn't originate from a system. It flowed from a person—Jesus Christ.

Many believers think grace is a concept or a principle. But grace is more than that—it is a person, embodied and revealed in Jesus. When He stepped onto the scene, everything changed. The law demanded perfection. Jesus provided it. The law exposed sin. Jesus erased it. Under the law, people lived in fear of judgment. Under Jesus, they encountered the kindness of a Savior who didn't just overlook sin, but bore it in His own body. Grace isn't leniency—it's divine empowerment wrapped in love.

This contrast between the law and grace is not about God's mood swings between covenants. It's about progression—from shadow to substance. The law came through Moses as a type, a foreshadowing of what was to come. But grace came through Jesus as the fulfillment of everything the law pointed toward. Where the law was rigid, Jesus was relational. Where the law condemned, Jesus restored. And through Him, the grace of God became tangible, accessible, and life-changing.

So let me ask: Are you still living as if you're under Moses, or have you come to know grace through Jesus? The difference between those two approaches will determine whether you live in condemnation or freedom, striving or rest, distance or intimacy.

Focus Point

"For the law was given through Moses, but grace and truth came through Jesus Christ." (John 1:17, NKJV)

This verse is a clear dividing line between two covenants. The law was a system—grace is a person. The law revealed our need for God—grace reveals God's heart toward us. Jesus didn't discard truth; He brought grace with it. Together, grace and truth provide a new way of living—one anchored in relationship rather than religion, in freedom rather than fear. Jesus didn't bring a better version of the law—He brought something completely new.

Main Theme

The theme of this chapter is simple yet revolutionary: Grace came through Jesus Christ, not through performance, sacrifice, or religious systems. The Mosaic Law served its purpose—to expose sin and point to the need for a Savior. But it could never save. Only Jesus could. Grace is not soft on sin—it's strong enough to conquer it. Through Christ, grace is now the means by which we are saved, empowered, and transformed. Grace is not just a message—it's a Man.

Grace didn't come from a system. Grace came from a Savior.

Key Scriptures

- *"For what the law could not do in that it was weak through the flesh, God did by sending His own Son..."* (Romans 8:3, NKJV)
- *"And of His fullness we have all received, and grace for grace."* (John 1:16, NKJV)
- *"For sin shall not have dominion over you, for you are not under law but under grace."* (Romans 6:14, NKJV)

Key Points

- **Grace Replaced the Law as the Covenant Foundation** The law served its purpose, but it was never the final plan. Grace is the new covenant standard.
- **Grace Came as a Person, Not a Policy** Jesus didn't bring a new system—He embodied grace. He is the source and expression of it.
- **Truth Was Not Abandoned—It Was Fulfilled** Jesus brought both grace and truth, showing us that freedom doesn't discard righteousness—it completes it.
- **The Law Could Reveal Sin, but Only Grace Could Remove It** The law exposed our inability; Jesus overcame it and gave us His righteousness.
- **Grace Empowers Holiness** Grace doesn't permit sin—it empowers victory over it through the indwelling life of Christ.
- **The Law Could Not Produce Relationship** Only grace, through Jesus, brings us into intimacy with the Father, not just obedience to rules.
- **Living Under Grace Brings Rest, Not Apathy** When you live under grace, you're no longer striving for God's approval—you're responding from it.

Journaling Questions

This chapter calls every believer to re-evaluate the covenant they're living under. Journaling through these truths helps you identify whether you've truly received the grace of Jesus, or whether you're still functioning under a mixture of law and grace. Many Christians intellectually affirm grace but live emotionally as if they're still trying to meet the demands of the law.

As you reflect and write, the Holy Spirit will begin to expose any remnants of legalism, fear, or performance-based mindsets that still linger. Journaling invites you to lay those burdens down and embrace the Person of grace—Jesus Christ. It helps move grace from concept to connection, from theory to encounter.

Law or Grace?

Am I still trying to earn God's acceptance through rules and performance, or have I received His grace through Jesus?

_____
_____
_____
_____
_____
_____
_____
_____

Grace as a Person

Do I see grace as a concept or as the person of Jesus Christ? How does that affect my relationship with Him?

_____
_____
_____
_____
_____
_____

Mixture of Covenants

Have I unintentionally mixed law and grace in how I live or lead others? What does the Word say about that?

_____
_____
_____
_____
_____

Grace and Truth Together

Do I embrace both grace and truth in my life, or do I lean more toward one at the expense of the other?

_____
_____
_____
_____
_____
_____
_____

Walking with Jesus, Not Moses

In what ways can I begin walking more closely with Jesus and less under the weight of law-based living?

_____
_____
_____
_____
_____
_____
_____

Actionable Steps

Identify Legalistic Patterns
Ask the Holy Spirit to show you one area of your life where you're still living under a "law mindset." Write it down and renounce it in prayer.

Personalize Grace
Spend time reading through the Gospels this week, observing how Jesus embodied grace. Journal what you learn about Him.

Declare Your Covenant

Each morning, declare: "I live under grace, not law. Jesus fulfilled what I could never do. I walk in freedom, not fear."

Personal Reflection

Grace is not soft. It's not weak. And it's not abstract. Grace has a name—Jesus. When you understand that grace came through Him, you stop trying to fit the New Covenant into Old Covenant thinking. You begin to walk not as a slave trying to obey, but as a child responding to love. Grace changes everything—not because it ignores truth, but because it fulfills it in the person of Christ.

This chapter calls you to leave behind performance and step into Person—to trade striving for surrender, fear for faith, and law for life. You are no longer under Moses. You are in Christ. Grace has come. And with it, the truth that you are deeply loved, fully forgiven, and completely free.

Do I live daily from the grace Jesus brought, or from the law Moses delivered? Am I relating to God through Christ or through performance? Am I ready to live under the Person of Grace—not just the principles of religion?

_____
_____
_____
_____
_____
_____
_____
_____
_____
_____
_____
_____
_____
_____
_____
_____

Closing Prayer: *Jesus, You are Grace. Thank You for doing what the law could never do—making a way for me to be right with the Father. Forgive me for every time I've lived under rules instead of Your relationship. I receive the fullness of grace that came through You. Help me walk in that truth every day. In Your name I pray, amen.*

Chapter 8

Grace Is a Rest

"There remains therefore a rest for the people of God. For he who has entered His rest has himself also ceased from his works as God did from His." (Hebrews 4:9-10, NKJV)

Years ago, I found myself in a season of spiritual exhaustion. I was doing all the right things—preaching, praying, studying, and serving—yet inside, I was tired. Worn out. Frustrated. I felt like I was always chasing approval from God, as though my performance determined His nearness. One day, while reading Hebrews, I came across a phrase that pierced through all my effort: "There remains a rest for the people of God." In that moment, I realized that grace wasn't just about being saved from sin—it was also an invitation to rest.

Many believers today are walking in salvation but not in rest. They've accepted Jesus but are still trying to prove their worth through endless striving. It's as if they've received the gift of grace but are afraid to actually sit down and enjoy it. But grace is not just the way we're saved—it's also the way we live. And when we truly understand grace, we stop performing and start abiding. We stop working for favor and begin living from favor.

Hebrews makes it clear that the people of Israel failed to enter God's rest, not because of a lack of effort, but because of unbelief. They could not accept that God had prepared something for them they didn't have to work to earn. It is the same today. Many struggle with grace because they are uncomfortable with the idea that God would freely give what we were never meant to earn. But grace invites us to cease from our own works and enter into the finished work of Christ.

So here's the question: Are you laboring under pressure to perform, or are you resting in the grace that was purchased for you? Real faith doesn't strive—it trusts. And where trust lives, rest begins.

Focus Point

"There remains therefore a rest for the people of God. For he who has entered His rest has himself also ceased from his works as God did from His." (Hebrews 4:9-10, NKJV)

This verse is a profound picture of grace in motion. God's rest is not inactivity—it is trust-driven surrender. Just as God ceased from His creation work on the seventh day, we are called to cease from striving to earn what has already been provided in Christ. This is not about laziness; it's about spiritual alignment. Entering God's rest is entering the full reality of grace.

Main Theme

The core message of this chapter is that grace is more than just the means to salvation—it is the lifestyle of rest that flows from trusting in Christ's finished work. This rest is not passive; it's powerful. It frees you from the cycle of striving and gives you the space to live fully from identity, not for it. When you live under grace, you no longer try to earn God's love, provision, or approval—they are already yours. Your job is not to work harder, but to believe deeper.

Rest is the rhythm of grace. When you trust the finished work of Jesus, your soul stops striving.

Key Scriptures

- *"Come to Me, all you who labor and are heavy laden, and I will give you rest."* (Matthew 11:28, NKJV)
- *"For we who have believed do enter that rest..."* (Hebrews 4:3, NKJV)
- *"Abide in Me, and I in you. As the branch cannot bear fruit of itself, unless it abides in the vine..."* (John 15:4, NKJV)

Key Points

- **Grace Produces Rest, Not Restlessness** When you truly understand grace, you stop striving to be enough and start resting in who God already says you are.
- **Rest Is Not Laziness—It's Trust** Ceasing from your own works doesn't mean you stop living or serving. It means your motivation shifts from earning to trusting.
- **Israel Missed the Rest Through Unbelief** The Promised Land wasn't just a place—it was a picture of spiritual rest. Their failure to believe cost them their inheritance.
- **Striving Is a Sign of Misunderstood Grace** If you constantly feel pressure to perform for God, you may be living under law instead of grace.
- **Abiding Is Resting** Jesus said to abide in Him, not to strive in Him. Fruitfulness comes from connection, not effort.
- **Grace Teaches You to Live From the Inside Out** When your soul is at rest, your life begins to align with the Spirit instead of reacting to pressure or fear.
- **Faith Is the Doorway to Rest** You don't enter God's rest by behavior—you enter by belief. Trusting in the finished work opens the gate.

Journaling Questions

This chapter offers one of the most transformative invitations in all of Scripture: to live from a place of grace-filled rest. Journaling through these truths helps you identify areas where you're still operating under pressure or performance. It allows the Holy Spirit to reveal whether you're laboring under law or living under grace.

As you reflect and write, don't be surprised if hidden motives and mindsets surface—things you've carried unknowingly that drive you to earn, prove, or achieve what God has already given. Journaling becomes a place of recalibration. It's where your soul learns to breathe again.

SOUL CHECK

Am I truly at rest in my relationship with God, or am I constantly striving to prove myself?

___

THE NATURE OF MY WORK

Are my spiritual activities rooted in grace and joy, or driven by guilt and fear?

___

BELIEVING VS. ACHIEVING

Where in my life have I prioritized achieving over simply believing?

___

Entering the Rest

What would change in my day-to-day life if I fully entered into the rest Jesus offers?

_____
_____
_____
_____
_____
_____
_____

Grace as Lifestyle

How can I let grace redefine my pace, my purpose, and my posture?

_____
_____
_____
_____
_____
_____
_____

Actionable Steps

Call a Time-Out
Take 30 minutes this week to rest—not just physically, but spiritually. Sit with God. Don't perform. Just receive. Let that moment reset your pace.

Replace Striving With Surrender
Identify one area where you've been trying to make things happen through pressure or control. Hand it back to God. Write a declaration of surrender.

Establish a Rest Rhythm
Create a rhythm in your week that includes intentional space for spiritual rest—whether through worship, reflection, or simply being still before God.

Personal Reflection

We are a generation running on spiritual fumes, constantly trying to do for God what He already finished. But the grace that saved you is the grace that sustains you. You don't have to work your way to peace. You simply enter in. Grace invites you to sit down in a finished work, to breathe deeply, and to stop fighting for what's already been won.

This is the heart of rest—not absence of activity, but absence of anxiety. Not doing nothing, but doing everything from a place of confidence and connection. You are not abandoned. You are not evaluated by your hustle. You are held, loved, and welcomed into rest.

Am I willing to lay down the weight of performance? Have I let grace become my rhythm? What would change if I truly believed the work was already finished?

Closing Prayer: *Father, thank You for the rest that comes from grace. I surrender my striving, my proving, and my pressure. Teach me to live from Your finished work. Let my soul abide in You. Help me walk in the rhythm of grace—not as a duty, but as my daily delight. In Jesus' name, amen.*

Chapter 9

Defining Moments

"See, I have set before you today life and good, death and evil... therefore choose life, that both you and your descendants may live." (Deuteronomy 30:15, 19, NKJV)

There are moments in life that define us. I remember one such moment when I stood at a spiritual crossroads. Everything I had believed, every sermon I had preached, suddenly faced a challenge. It wasn't just an emotional storm or a physical trial—it was a defining moment that demanded a decision. Would I believe God's Word despite my feelings, or would I let circumstances rewrite my theology? That moment didn't just shape the outcome of that season—it shaped me. It became a line in the sand.

Every believer will face these kinds of defining moments. These are not merely hard times—they are decision points. Moments where the voice of grace calls you to trust deeper, walk bolder, and stand firmer than ever before. These moments are invitations. Not to destruction, but to destiny. God doesn't orchestrate tragedy, but He does meet us in every trial with a choice: will you believe My Word, or will you cave to the pressure?

The children of Israel had countless defining moments. Standing at the edge of the Promised Land, they had the choice to believe the promise or be swallowed by fear. Ten chose fear. Two chose faith. The result? An entire generation missed their inheritance, not because God changed, but because they did not mix His Word with faith. Defining moments don't just shape outcomes—they reveal beliefs. What you believe in those moments determines what you experience.

So let me ask you: What are you choosing in your defining moments? Are you choosing life or death, faith or fear, grace or works? These moments are more than turning points—they are revealing points. And in them, God extends His grace—not just to save you, but to shape you.

Focus Point

"See, I have set before you today life and good, death and evil... therefore choose life, that both you and your descendants may live." (Deuteronomy 30:15, 19, NKJV)

This verse frames the gravity of our choices. In every defining moment, God gives us an invitation—to choose life. This is not about law; it's about alignment. The choices we make affect more than just ourselves—they touch generations. Choosing to believe God's Word over our fears releases life, not only to us but through us. Every moment becomes an opportunity to trust the grace extended to us.

Main Theme

The primary theme of this chapter is that defining moments shape our spiritual journey and must be met with faith in God's grace and promises. These moments are not obstacles—they are invitations. They separate those who hear the Word from those who believe it. Every believer faces moments when the truth of the Word must overrule emotion, pressure, or popular opinion. In those moments, grace empowers the right choice, but we must respond with faith.

A defining moment is not just about what happens—it's about what you decide to believe.

Key Scriptures

- *"For indeed the gospel was preached to us as well as to them; but the word which they heard did not profit them, not being mixed with faith in those who heard it."* (Hebrews 4:2, NKJV)
- *"So I have come down to deliver them out of the hand of the Egyptians... Come now, therefore, and I will send you to Pharaoh..."* (Exodus 3:8, 10, NKJV)

- *"Trust in the Lord with all your heart, and lean not on your own understanding; in all your ways acknowledge Him, and He shall direct your paths." (Proverbs 3:5–6, NKJV)*

Key Points

- **Defining Moments Are Crossroads** These are not just trials—they are turning points where decisions must align with truth, not emotion.
- **You Must Mix the Word with Faith** Hearing God's Word isn't enough. It must be combined with belief and action to produce results.
- **God's Grace Meets You at the Moment of Decision** You are never alone in your defining moments. Grace empowers you to choose rightly.
- **Fear Can Rob You of Your Inheritance** Just like Israel, choosing fear in a defining moment can delay or destroy what God intended for you.
- **Faith Is a Choice, Not a Feeling** Waiting for your feelings to line up will keep you stuck. Faith acts on truth in spite of emotion.
- **Defining Moments Reveal What You Really Believe** What you choose under pressure shows the depth of your trust in God and His Word.
- **God Uses These Moments to Shape Destiny** Every defining moment is a setup for growth, promotion, and deeper intimacy with God—if you choose well.

Journaling Questions

This chapter invites you to look back at the forked roads of your life and examine how you've responded—and to prepare for the ones to come. Journaling helps clarify what those moments revealed about your trust in God and where growth is still needed. Every defining moment is both a test and a training opportunity.

As you reflect, the Holy Spirit will begin to highlight past decisions, not to shame you, but to illuminate patterns. You'll also begin to see how grace was present—even when you missed it. Journaling creates space for fresh resolve and a deeper reliance on God's Word, preparing you for the defining moments ahead.

Looking Back with Clarity

What defining moments have shaped my spiritual walk? How did I respond—by faith or fear?

_____
_____
_____
_____
_____
_____
_____
_____

The Role of Belief

Did I truly mix God's Word with faith in those moments, or did I default to what was familiar?

_____
_____
_____
_____
_____
_____
_____

Rewriting the Narrative

Where do I need to revisit a past decision and receive healing or re-alignment with God's truth?

_____
_____
_____
_____
_____
_____
_____

Choosing Grace Over Pressure

In what areas of my life am I still striving instead of trusting? What is God calling me to believe today?

_____
_____
_____
_____
_____
_____
_____

Preparing for What's Ahead

How can I better prepare to stand in faith the next time I encounter a defining moment?

_____
_____
_____
_____
_____
_____
_____

Actionable Steps

Revisit a Defining Moment
Write about a past defining moment. Identify what you believed at the time and what God was trying to teach you. Ask Him to redeem that moment fully.

Practice Choosing Life
Start your day by verbally choosing life. Say: "Today I choose life, I choose grace, I choose to believe God's Word above all else."

Create a Faith Response Plan
Pick one area where you're facing a decision. Write down a Scripture, a declaration, and a corresponding action that reflect faith.

Personal Reflection

Life isn't defined by comfort—it's defined by choices. And the most critical choices come when everything is on the line. In those moments, what you believe about God, grace, and truth becomes more than theology—it becomes your foundation. You will either stand or fall on what you believe in your defining moments.

But God is not testing you to trap you—He's calling you higher. These moments are not just trials—they're training grounds. And you don't walk into them alone. Grace goes before you, beside you, and within you, empowering your every choice. The question is, will you trust Him enough to choose life?

What have I believed about God in my defining moments? Have I allowed fear to determine my steps—or has faith led the way? Am I ready to meet my next defining moment with grace and truth, trusting God fully?

Closing Prayer: *Father, thank You that You are with me in every defining moment. I repent for the times I let fear make my decisions. Teach me to mix Your Word with faith. Help me to choose life when pressure rises and to trust that grace empowers my every step. I commit to follow You—not feelings, not fear, but Your truth. In Jesus' name, amen.*

Chapter 10

Your Destiny Depends on Grace

"But by the grace of God I am what I am, and His grace toward me was not in vain; but I labored more abundantly than they all, yet not I, but the grace of God which was with me." (1 Corinthians 15:10, NKJV)

I once heard a man say, "I pulled myself up by my own bootstraps." He wore it like a badge of honor. But in the Kingdom of God, that badge holds no value. The truth is, no one fulfills their God-given destiny by willpower alone. I've seen people with talent, passion, and drive still fall short of what they were called to do because they misunderstood one vital truth: your destiny doesn't depend on your strength—it depends on God's grace.

The Apostle Paul understood this better than anyone. He didn't downplay the call on his life, but he never credited himself for his success. He recognized that everything he accomplished flowed from grace. He worked hard, yes—but not to earn destiny. He worked because grace empowered him. Grace was the force behind the mission. And that same grace is what will get you to your destination—not just anointing, not just discipline, but divine enablement that flows from the heart of God.

When we begin to understand that our destiny is grace-dependent, we stop striving and start aligning. Grace opens doors that hustle can't. It gives favor that education can't buy. It equips us to go beyond what we're naturally capable of. But here's the key: grace must be received. If you try to fulfill your calling in your own strength, you'll burn out. If you rest in grace, you'll run with endurance. Grace doesn't just forgive your past—it fuels your future.

So I ask: Are you pursuing your calling through your own efforts or depending on the power of grace? Your destiny isn't about proving yourself. It's about yielding to the One who called you and walking in the divine strength He provides.

Focus Point

"But by the grace of God I am what I am... yet not I, but the grace of God which was with me." (1 Corinthians 15:10, NKJV)

This verse is Paul's confession—and it should be ours. He didn't minimize his work, but he magnified the source. Grace shaped his identity, empowered his mission, and sustained his labor. Destiny isn't fulfilled by grit alone. It's accomplished through grace. Paul worked harder than anyone, but it was God's power working through him that made it effective. Grace doesn't eliminate effort—it empowers it.

Main Theme

The central message of this chapter is that grace is not just the entry point to salvation—it is the sustaining power for destiny. You were not created to live out God's calling by natural strength or religious duty. Grace is the supernatural supply that makes your assignment possible. It's not a soft crutch—it's a divine force. Without grace, destiny becomes a burden. With grace, destiny becomes a journey of joy, favor, and fulfillment.

Your destiny is not achieved by effort alone—it's fulfilled by grace flowing through surrendered obedience.

Key Scriptures

- *"Not that we are sufficient of ourselves to think of anything as being from ourselves, but our sufficiency is from God."* (2 Corinthians 3:5, NKJV)
- *"And God is able to make all grace abound toward you, that you, always having all sufficiency in all things, may have an abundance for every good work."* (2 Corinthians 9:8, NKJV)

- *"Being confident of this very thing, that He who has begun a good work in you will complete it..."* (Philippians 1:6, NKJV)

Key Points

- **Grace Establishes Identity** You are who you are because of grace, not because of effort or background.
- **Grace Empowers Calling** Every spiritual assignment requires supernatural empowerment—grace is that power.
- **Grace and Responsibility Work Together** Grace does not cancel diligence—it inspires and sustains it.
- **Destiny Outside of Grace Is Exhausting** When you operate in your own strength, burnout and frustration follow.
- **Grace Must Be Received and Recognized** Many have grace available but fail to walk in it because they don't recognize or honor it.
- **Grace Doesn't Eliminate Work—It Energizes It** Paul said he worked more than anyone, but it wasn't from effort—it was grace flowing through him.
- **God Finishes What He Starts** Your calling isn't up to you alone. Grace began it, and grace will complete it.

Journaling Questions

Journaling through this chapter creates space to evaluate whether you're walking in grace or grinding in your own strength. Destiny without grace becomes pressure. But when grace is your fuel, you begin to move with confidence and peace. Reflection will help you trace whether your current pace and posture are aligned with God's empowerment—or rooted in striving.

As you journal, you'll begin to identify places where pride, performance, or pressure have crept into your pursuit of calling. You'll also rediscover moments where grace carried you—moments you couldn't have planned or executed on your own. Let those reflections draw you into a deeper dependence on God's sustaining power.

Self-Reliance vs. God-Dependence

Am I trying to fulfill my calling by my own strength, or have I truly surrendered to the grace of God?

_____
_____
_____
_____
_____
_____
_____

Recognizing Grace

Can I identify specific times where grace carried me farther than my effort ever could?

_____
_____
_____
_____
_____
_____

Effort or Empowerment?

Is my work for the Lord driven by pressure or empowered by joy and grace?

_____
_____
_____
_____
_____

Signs of Burnout

Have I been spiritually or emotionally exhausted lately? Could it be a sign that I've drifted from grace?

_____
_____
_____
_____
_____
_____

Aligning With Grace

What practical steps can I take this week to rely more on grace and less on effort?

_____
_____
_____
_____
_____
_____

Actionable Steps

Write Your Grace Confession
Take Paul's words in 1 Corinthians 15:10 and rewrite them as a personal declaration of your dependence on grace.

Pause and Realign
Before making any major decision or pursuing a new goal, pause and ask: "Am I doing this in grace or in pressure?" Let the answer guide your next step.
covenant.

Celebrate Past Grace

Journal or share a testimony of a time when God's grace made the impossible possible in your life. Let it build faith for what's ahead.

Personal Reflection

You were never meant to fulfill your destiny through willpower. The calling on your life was born of grace and must be walked out in grace. There is freedom in knowing that you are not the source—God is. Your destiny doesn't rise and fall on your performance. It flourishes when you rest in His power and walk in His provision.

Let grace redefine your path. Don't strive to make it happen—yield to the One who already authored your story. When grace leads, burdens lift. When grace empowers, progress accelerates. This is not a call to ease, but a call to alignment. Your role is not to manufacture destiny—it's to walk with the One who already finished it.

Am I laboring apart from grace or partnering with it? Do I trust that grace is enough to sustain and fulfill my calling? Am I ready to let grace fuel every step of my destiny journey?

Closing Prayer: *Father, thank You for the grace that not only saved me but sustains me. I surrender my striving and lean into Your divine strength. Let grace empower my calling, define my work, and fuel my every step. I am who I am by Your grace—and I choose to live and labor in it daily. In Jesus' name, amen.*

Chapter 11

Grace Is Not a License to Sin

"What shall we say then? Shall we continue in sin that grace may abound? Certainly not! How shall we who died to sin live any longer in it?" (Romans 6:1-2, NKJV)

I once spoke with a man who said, "Well, if grace covers all my sin tomorrow, I'll just sin a bit more today so I can enjoy more grace." At first I thought he was joking. But the Apostle Paul addresses this very mindset—and he slams the door on it. Grace is not a permission slip to live however we please; it's the power that breaks sin's grip. Once we understand that we've died to sin and been raised to newness of life in Christ, we see that grace calls us into holiness, not lawlessness.

Grace covers our past, but it also empowers our present and future. It doesn't remove the call to obedience; it equips us to obey. When we grasp that the same grace that forgives is the grace that sanctifies, we stop treating sin as a strategy. We start treating sin as what it is—an offense against a holy God. Grace then becomes the fuel for victorious living, not the excuse for destructive living.

So I ask: Do you view grace as a license or as the strength to say no? Your answer will determine whether you live in bondage to sin's cycle or in the freedom of Christ's deliverance.

Focus Point

"Shall we continue in sin that grace may abound? Certainly not!" (Romans 6:1–2, NKJV)

Paul's emphatic "Certainly not!" makes it clear: grace is not an invitation to sin. It's a call to live as those who have died to sin and risen into a new life. Grace doesn't nullify righteousness—it enforces it by giving us the power to overcome.

Main Theme

The main message of this chapter is that grace empowers believers to live victoriously over sin, not to indulge in it. Grace covers our failures, but it also equips us to walk in newness of life. Understanding this protects us from lawlessness masquerading as freedom. True grace always leads to a transformed life.

Grace forgives. Grace transforms. It is never an excuse for sin.

Key Scriptures

- *"For sin shall not have dominion over you, for you are not under law but under grace."* (Romans 6:14, NKJV)
- *"Likewise you also, reckon yourselves to be dead indeed to sin, but alive to God in Christ Jesus our Lord."* (Romans 6:11, NKJV)
- *"How shall we who died to sin live any longer in it?"* (Romans 6:2, NKJV)

Key Points

- **Grace Is Not a Get-Out-of-Jail Card** Grace frees us from sin's penalty, but it also liberates us from sin's control.
- **Dead to Sin, Alive to God** Because we died with Christ, sin no longer defines us. We are called to live in that reality.
- **Grace and Obedience Coexist** Grace empowers obedience. True freedom in Christ always bears fruit.

- **Lawlessness Is Not Freedom** Confusing grace with lawlessness enslaves us. Genuine freedom transforms our desires.
- **Grace Teaches Us to Say No** Rather than using grace to excuse sin, we use grace to resist temptation.
- **Holiness Is Grace's Hallmark** The evidence of grace in our life is a growing likeness to Christ.
- **Grace Produces Repentance** When we grasp the cost of grace, sin becomes a sorrow, not a strategy.

Journaling Questions

Journaling through this chapter helps you identify any misconceptions about grace that enable sin. Reflection exposes where sin has crept back under the guise of freedom. This process invites the Spirit to renew your mind with the truth that grace calls you to holiness, not lawlessness.

Grace or License?

Have I ever used grace as justification for ongoing sin? Where?

_____
_____
_____
_____
_____

Transformation vs. Permission

Do I expect grace to change me, or do I see it as permission to remain the same?

_____
_____
_____
_____
_____

Counting Myself Dead

Do I truly reckon myself dead to sin and alive to God? What would that look like today?

_____
_____
_____
_____
_____
_____
_____

Fruit of Grace

Where in my life is grace producing obedience and holiness—and where is it not?

_____
_____
_____
_____
_____
_____
_____

Repentance Path

What sin have I minimized under the banner of grace? How will I respond now?

_____
_____
_____
_____
_____
_____
_____

Actionable Steps

Confess and Replace

Identify one ongoing sin you've excused with grace. Confess it, then declare: "By grace, I choose holiness."

Memorize Romans 6

Commit Romans 6:1–14 to memory. Let it shape your understanding of grace and sin.

Grace-Fueled Accountability

Partner with a trusted friend. Share your confession and ask them to encourage your walk in holiness under grace.

Personal Reflection

Grace is never an excuse for sin. It's the very power that breaks sin's chains. When you see grace as the catalyst for transformation, not the cover for rebellion, you step into true freedom. Sin loses its appeal, and Christ's life becomes your pattern.

Am I living under grace's power or law's shadow? Do I know what it means to be dead to sin and alive to God? Am I ready to let grace produce holiness in every part of my life?

Closing Prayer: *Lord, forgive me for using grace as a license to sin. I choose to live as one who died to sin and rose in You. Empower me with Your grace to walk in holiness, honor You in my choices, and reflect Christ in all I do. In Jesus' name, amen.*

Chapter 12

Grace Is Not Automatic

"We then, as workers together with Him also plead with you not to receive the grace of God in vain." (2 Corinthians 6:1, NKJV)

Years ago, I heard a believer say, "Well, God's grace will just take care of it." The situation they were referring to involved a pattern of destructive choices they were making without any plan to change. What struck me was not just their assumption but their passive confidence that grace would somehow clean up a mess they refused to confront. It sounded spiritual—but it was deeply misguided. That moment revealed a widespread misunderstanding: grace is not automatic. It must be received, believed, and acted upon.

God's grace is abundant, but it is not passive. Scripture tells us that we can receive the grace of God in vain. That means grace can be poured out, but not accessed. Offered, but not applied. Just like the children of Israel, who heard the Word but didn't mix it with faith, we can be surrounded by the potential of grace and never experience its power if we remain indifferent or disobedient.

Grace must be partnered with humility, faith, and obedience. It's not something that just "kicks in" like spiritual autopilot. If that were the case, no one would ever fall into sin, miss their destiny, or resist the will of God. But we do. Why? Because grace must be received intentionally and stewarded wisely. It's not an automatic download—it's a divine invitation.

So here's the question: Are you assuming grace will do what only surrender can activate? Have you received it in vain by hearing the Word and doing nothing with it? This chapter is your wake-up call—grace is available, but it's not automatic.

Focus Point

"We then... plead with you not to receive the grace of God in vain." (2 Corinthians 6:1, NKJV)

This verse proves grace can be misapplied or even wasted. Paul wasn't questioning whether grace had been given—he was warning believers not to receive it passively. Grace demands response. It requires faith, humility, and yieldedness. It can be resisted, ignored, or squandered. But when received rightly, it transforms.

Main Theme

The main theme of this chapter is that grace must be intentionally received and actively applied. It is available to all, but not accessed by all. Grace is powerful, but it is not imposed. It requires cooperation—faith, surrender, and action. Many believers assume that grace will just work in the background of their lives like a spiritual operating system. But grace requires your attention. It's a divine partnership, not a divine override.

Grace is not automatic—it's an invitation that must be answered.

Key Scriptures

- *"But He gives more grace. Therefore He says: 'God resists the proud, but gives grace to the humble.'"* (James 4:6, NKJV)
- *"Looking carefully lest anyone fall short of the grace of God..."* (Hebrews 12:15, NKJV)
- *"Therefore do not be unwise, but understand what the will of the Lord is."* (Ephesians 5:17, NKJV)

Key Points

- **Grace Can Be Received in Vain** You can hear the message, quote the verses, and still waste the grace if you never apply it.

- **Grace Must Be Mixed with Faith** God provides grace, but you must respond in belief and action for it to produce results.
- **Pride Blocks the Flow of Grace** God gives grace to the humble. A proud heart forfeits what grace offers.
- **Disobedience Disqualifies Grace's Effects** Grace doesn't cover willful rebellion. It empowers obedience—but only when we yield to it.
- **Grace Can Be Resisted** Just like the Holy Spirit, grace can be grieved, resisted, or rejected.
- **Assumption Isn't Activation** Believing grace exists is not the same as walking in its power. Activation comes through humility and surrender.
- **Grace Responds to Submission** You don't earn grace—but you must yield to it. Submission is the landing strip for grace to work in your life.

Journaling Questions

Journaling through this chapter will expose passive mindsets that have dulled your spiritual growth. Many believers assume that grace is just working in the background, like a system they never have to engage. But reflection helps you see whether grace has become a neglected theory instead of a living power.

This journaling process gives space for honest evaluation. Where have you assumed grace would "just happen"? Where have you resisted correction, counsel, or change? Let this chapter be the catalyst for renewed engagement with the grace of God—intentional, personal, and powerful.

Recognizing Passivity

Have I received God's grace in vain by hearing truth but not applying it?

_____
_____
_____
_____
_____
_____

Evaluating Response

What areas of my life show that I've responded to grace with faith and obedience?

_____
_____
_____
_____
_____
_____

Humble Posture

Am I walking in humility, where grace can flow freely? Or have I blocked it with pride or resistance?

_____
_____
_____
_____
_____
_____

Assumption vs. Activation

Where have I assumed grace would work automatically instead of partnering with it?

_____
_____
_____
_____
_____
_____

Course Correction

What's one area where I need to intentionally receive and activate grace starting today?

_____
_____
_____
_____
_____
_____

Actionable Steps

Pray for Fresh Sensitivity
Ask the Holy Spirit to make you aware of where you've received grace in vain. Write down what He reveals and commit to responding.

Take One Grace-Fueled Action
Choose one area—like forgiveness, generosity, purity, or surrender—and act on it, knowing grace will empower, not just instruct.

Confess and Reset
If you've neglected grace in any area, confess it. Declare: "Grace is not automatic in me—I choose to walk in it now."

Personal Reflection

Grace is not just God's gift—it's God's invitation. And like every invitation, it requires a response. You cannot drift into maturity. You cannot assume transformation. Grace must be stewarded, embraced, and pursued. You are not waiting on grace—grace is waiting on you.

Let this be your moment of re-engagement. Let your heart respond afresh to grace's call. Not with striving, but with surrender. Not with guilt, but with readiness. Grace is powerful, available, and active—but only if you say yes to its work in you.

Have I allowed grace to sit dormant in my life? Am I responding to grace with action and surrender? Am I ready to live as one who values the power and purpose of grace?

Closing Prayer: *Father, I repent for every moment I received Your grace in vain. Thank You for not withholding it, even when I ignored it. I choose today to respond, to activate, and to obey. I open my heart fully to grace—not just as a doctrine, but as a power. Let it work in me, shape me, and lead me forward. In Jesus' name, amen.*

Chapter 13

Growing in Grace

"But grow in the grace and knowledge of our Lord and Savior Jesus Christ. To Him be the glory both now and forever. Amen." (2 Peter 3:18, NKJV)

I remember looking at a sapling in my backyard years ago. It was barely a few feet tall, vulnerable to the wind and weather. But I knew it wouldn't stay that way. With time, sun, water, and deep roots, it would grow into a mighty tree. In the same way, God spoke to me through that tree about grace. Just as trees don't spring up fully mature, grace doesn't manifest fully formed in our lives overnight. It must grow. It must deepen. It must be nurtured intentionally.

Some believe grace is a static, one-time gift you receive at salvation—and in part, that's true. But Peter's words ring loud: "Grow in grace." That means grace is not just a starting point; it's a journey. You don't graduate from grace. You grow in it. Just like you mature in wisdom, love, and faith, you must mature in your understanding and application of grace. This is where many believers miss it. They camp out at the place of forgiveness, never advancing into the empowering force that grace truly is.

Growing in grace transforms you. It changes how you think, how you speak, how you live, and how you respond to others. It's not just about receiving grace for yourself—it's about extending it. It's about learning to walk in what you've received so fully that it overflows to those around you. The more you grow in grace, the more you grow into the likeness of Christ.

So I ask you today: Are you growing in grace—or just coasting in your Christian walk? Maturity doesn't happen by accident. It requires intentionality. And grace is the soil where your spiritual life takes root and bears fruit.

Focus Point

"But grow in the grace and knowledge of our Lord and Savior Jesus Christ." (2 Peter 3:18, NKJV)

This verse is not a suggestion—it's a command. It reveals that grace is not just received; it's developed. Growth in grace is tied directly to growing in the knowledge of Jesus. As you deepen your relationship with Him, grace becomes more active, more visible, and more powerful in your life. You are not meant to stay in the same place. Grace is designed to expand.

Main Theme

The central message of this chapter is that grace is not stagnant—it grows. We must move beyond receiving grace into maturing in it. Growing in grace means learning to rely more on God, less on ourselves, and allowing grace to shape every area of our lives—speech, thoughts, reactions, and character. True spiritual maturity isn't just about knowledge—it's about walking more fully in grace.

Grace is not only a foundation—it's the framework for spiritual growth.

Key Scriptures

- *"And of His fullness we have all received, and grace for grace."* (John 1:16, NKJV)
- *"For the grace of God that brings salvation has appeared to all men, teaching us..."* (Titus 2:11–12, NKJV)
- *"Let your speech always be with grace, seasoned with salt..."* (Colossians 4:6, NKJV)

Key Points

- **Grace Is Meant to Grow** Like a seed, grace is planted at salvation—but it must be cultivated to mature.
- **Spiritual Growth Requires Grace** You cannot grow spiritually apart from grace. It empowers you to grow beyond your limitations.

- **Grace Teaches, Not Just Saves** Grace doesn't just forgive—it instructs, disciplines, and develops Christlike character.
- **Growth Is Not Automatic** You must intentionally pursue growth in grace through the Word, prayer, and surrender.
- **Grace Impacts Every Area** From your thoughts to your speech to your relationships, growing in grace transforms your entire life.
- **The More You Know Jesus, the More Grace Flows** Grace and the knowledge of Christ are intertwined. Knowing Him more releases greater grace.
- **Mature Grace Extends to Others** As you grow in grace, you become a vessel of it—extending patience, mercy, and kindness to those around you.

Journaling Questions

Journaling through this chapter will help you assess whether you're growing in grace or simply maintaining. Reflection creates space to evaluate how grace is shaping your actions, thoughts, and relationships. You'll begin to see whether grace is just a theological concept—or a transforming reality.

As you write, let the Holy Spirit reveal how grace has expanded in your life and where it still needs to take deeper root. Journaling becomes a mirror—not to condemn, but to encourage growth. Let grace be both your soil and your sustenance as you grow.

Assessing My Growth

In what ways have I grown in grace over the past year? What areas remain stagnant?

_____
_____
_____
_____
_____
_____
_____

Grace in My Reactions

Do I respond to pressure, conflict, or offense with grace—or with flesh?

_____
_____
_____
_____
_____
_____

Learning from Grace

What has grace taught me recently? How is it instructing me today?

_____
_____
_____
_____
_____
_____

Grace Toward Others

Am I extending grace as freely as I've received it? Who needs grace from me right now?

_____
_____
_____
_____
_____
_____

Intentionally Growing

What can I do today to intentionally cultivate deeper grace in my walk with Christ?

_____
_____
_____
_____
_____
_____

Actionable Steps

Track Your Growth
Write a one-page reflection on how grace has changed you in the past year. Celebrate progress and ask God for more.

Study Grace Intentionally
Spend the next week studying Scriptures about grace. Journal what the Holy Spirit reveals about how to grow in it.

Practice Giving Grace
Choose one person this week who has tested your patience. Extend grace to them intentionally —in speech, prayer, or kindness.

Personal Reflection

Growth doesn't happen by accident—and neither does growing in grace. You must choose to yield daily, to learn, to stretch, and to walk it out. Grace is not a finish line—it's a pathway. And every step you take in grace makes you more like Jesus.

Let grace be more than a message. Let it be your method. As you grow in grace, you will begin to see the fruit of transformation, the power of patience, and the beauty of Christlikeness in your everyday life. That is the mark of true maturity.

Am I still growing—or am I coasting? Is grace shaping my words, actions, and character? Am I willing to pursue growth in grace like never before?

Closing Prayer: *Lord Jesus, thank You for the grace that saved me—and the grace that grows me. I don't want to remain the same. Teach me to walk more fully in grace every day. Help me extend what I've received and live from Your strength. Grow me in grace and in the knowledge of who You are. In Your name I pray, amen.*

Chapter 14

How to Obtain Grace

"But He gives more grace. Therefore He says: 'God resists the proud, but gives grace to the humble."
(James 4:6, NKJV)

I'll never forget a moment in ministry when I felt completely overwhelmed. No amount of study, planning, or personal discipline could seem to lift the weight I was carrying. I wasn't in rebellion—I was simply worn down. So I did the only thing I knew to do: I humbled myself and cried out to God. It wasn't a polished prayer. It wasn't eloquent. But it was real. And in that moment, grace came rushing in like a wave. Strength returned. Peace settled in. And I understood a deeper truth than ever before—grace isn't random. It is given. And it is given to the humble.

The Bible makes it plain: there is a way to receive grace. It's not through striving or impressing God. It's through humility. Humility is not thinking less of yourself—it's thinking of yourself rightly in the light of who God is. It's admitting that you need Him, not just for salvation, but for every moment of every day. Grace flows where pride ends. It's not that God withholds grace from the proud to be harsh—it's that pride blocks the channel through which grace flows.

This principle is life-changing. The more you posture your heart in humility, the more grace God can entrust to you. It's not earned, but it is positioned for. That means grace doesn't just come to the gifted—it comes to the yielded. And the greater the humility, the greater the grace. Whether it's for forgiveness, power, wisdom, or strength—grace comes to those who bow low.

So the question is: Are you truly in position to receive more grace? Or has pride crept in through self-reliance, busyness, or performance? Grace is waiting—but it only flows to those who kneel.

Focus Point

"God resists the proud, but gives grace to the humble." (James 4:6, NKJV)

This verse is the gateway to obtaining grace. It reveals both the problem and the promise. Pride provokes resistance from God—not because He is cruel, but because pride rejects His help. But humility swings the door wide open for grace to enter. This is not just a theological truth—it's a spiritual law. If you want more grace, walk in more humility.

Main Theme

The core message of this chapter is that grace is freely given, but it must be intentionally obtained through humility and surrender. You don't earn grace by performance, but you position yourself to receive it by acknowledging your dependence on God. Pride blocks grace; humility unlocks it. This principle applies to every area of life—from salvation to daily strength, from spiritual gifts to godly relationships. The more humble you are, the more grace you'll receive.

You can't earn grace, but you can access more of it by bowing low.

Key Scriptures

- *"Let us therefore come boldly to the throne of grace, that we may obtain mercy and find grace to help in time of need."* (Hebrews 4:16, NKJV)
- *"Surely He scorns the scornful, but gives grace to the humble."* (Proverbs 3:34, NKJV)
- *"Humble yourselves in the sight of the Lord, and He will lift you up."* (James 4:10, NKJV)

Key Points

- **Grace Is Given to the Humble** You don't earn grace by good behavior. You receive it when you bow your heart before God.
- **Pride Resists God's Hand** God resists the proud—not because He is distant, but because pride refuses His help.
- **Humility Is the Position of Power** Humility doesn't weaken you—it makes you a candidate for supernatural strength.
- **The Throne of Grace Is Open** We are invited to come boldly to God's throne—not timidly, but confidently—when we are in need.
- **Grace Helps in Real-Time** Grace isn't just for salvation. It's for every moment of need—spiritual, emotional, physical.
- **Grace Is Sought, Not Assumed** Just because grace is available doesn't mean it's active in your life. You must come and receive.
- **Your Posture Determines Your Portion** The more you posture yourself in humility, the more grace can be poured into your life.

Journaling Questions

Journaling through this chapter invites you to reflect honestly on your posture before God. Many of us think we're walking in humility, but subtle pride can show up in independence, control, or resistance to correction. Journaling helps expose these blind spots—not to condemn, but to position you for more grace.

As you write, ask the Holy Spirit to reveal any areas where pride has hindered the flow of grace. Let this be a moment of surrender—not as a punishment, but as a pathway. Every time you humble yourself, you make more room for God's power to meet your weakness.

Grace Blockers

Have I been unknowingly resisting grace through pride or self-reliance?

_____
_____
_____
_____

Posture Check

What does humility look like in my daily life? Am I truly bowed before God in heart and will?

_____
_____
_____
_____
_____
_____

Coming to the Throne

Do I come boldly and regularly to the throne of grace? Or do I avoid it out of guilt or fear?

_____
_____
_____
_____
_____
_____

Receiving Help

In what areas do I need grace "to help in time of need"? Have I asked for it?

_____
_____
_____
_____
_____

Fresh Surrender

Where is God calling me to bow low so He can pour out fresh grace?

_____
_____
_____
_____
_____
_____

Actionable Steps

Name and Surrender
Write down one area where pride has blocked grace in your life. Confess it. Lay it down before God and ask for fresh grace.

Approach the Throne Boldly
Set aside 15 minutes this week to intentionally come to the "throne of grace." Bring your need before Him and ask for help without shame.

Practice Humility
Choose one action this week that reflects humility—whether it's asking for help, apologizing, or yielding in a conversation. Watch how grace flows into that moment.

Personal Reflection

Grace is not elusive. It's not reserved for the elite. It's waiting at the feet of those who bow. In a world that applauds self-sufficiency, heaven honors humility. You don't have to be the strongest or the smartest. You just have to be surrendered. And when you are, grace will meet you in ways you never imagined.

Let this truth reframe how you seek God. You don't have to perform. You simply have to come. And every time you do, He gives more grace. That's His promise. That's your invitation.

Am I resisting or receiving grace? Have I bowed low enough for more of Him? Am I ready to humble myself so that grace can have full access to my life?

Closing Prayer: *Lord, I humble myself before You today. I acknowledge my need. I confess any pride that has blocked Your grace. I come boldly to Your throne—not because I'm worthy, but because You are faithful. Pour out Your grace in every area of my life. Let humility be my posture and grace be my portion. In Jesus' name, amen.*

Chapter 15

Your Words Affect the Power of Grace

"Let no corrupt word proceed out of your mouth, but what is good for necessary edification, that it may impart grace to the hearers." (Ephesians 4:29, NKJV)

I was in a conversation once with a fellow minister who seemed discouraged. After just a few minutes of sharing, it was obvious why. Every sentence out of his mouth was saturated with negativity, doubt, and defeat. It wasn't that his situation was hopeless—it was that his words had drained the atmosphere of any faith. I could sense in my spirit how this steady stream of negative confession was cutting him off from the grace that God had already made available to help him. And that's when it hit me: our words don't just describe our reality—they shape what grace can do in our lives.

The Bible tells us clearly that grace can be imparted—or hindered—through the words we speak. Words aren't neutral. They carry spiritual weight. They are either aligned with God's truth or in opposition to it. When our speech is full of fear, doubt, gossip, or complaint, we not only pollute the atmosphere—we limit the access grace has to flow freely in and through us. But when we speak life, when our mouths agree with God's Word, grace becomes active. It imparts strength, peace, healing, and hope.

This is why we are warned not to grieve the Holy Spirit with our words. What you say affects more than your mood—it affects your momentum. Grace flows where faith speaks. It responds to truth, not to drama. And that's not just for public preaching—it's for personal living. Every believer must learn that their tongue can be a conduit for grace or a cork that stops it.

So I challenge you: What are your words creating right now? Are they making room for grace to build, restore, and empower? Or are they blocking the very thing God has provided to help you?

Focus Point

"Let no corrupt word proceed out of your mouth... that it may impart grace to the hearers." (Ephesians 4:29, NKJV)

This verse links the grace of God directly to the words we speak. It reveals that our speech is not only about communication—it's about impartation. What comes out of your mouth can either release grace or corrupt the atmosphere. Our tongues are not just expressive—they're prophetic. They declare what we believe, and they either align with the flow of grace or restrict it.

Main Theme

The core message of this chapter is that your words have the power to either release or resist the grace of God in your life and the lives of others. Speech is spiritual. It's not merely emotional or circumstantial—it's a vessel. You must learn to speak in alignment with grace so that your words build faith, invite the Holy Spirit's presence, and activate divine help. Loose lips don't just sink ships—they silence grace.

Words matter. Speak in agreement with grace, and grace will move in agreement with you.

Key Scriptures

- *"Death and life are in the power of the tongue, and those who love it will eat its fruit."* (Proverbs 18:21, NKJV)
- *"For out of the abundance of the heart the mouth speaks."* (Matthew 12:34, NKJV)
- *"By your words you will be justified, and by your words you will be condemned."* (Matthew 12:37, NKJV)

Key Points

- **Your Mouth Is a Grace Channel** Your words either create a runway for grace to land or a wall that blocks its flow.
- **Grace-Filled Speech Builds Others** When your words edify, they release grace to your hearers and draw the presence of the Holy Spirit.
- **Negative Talk Limits Grace's Effect** Complaining, gossip, or unbelief grieves the Spirit and disrupts grace's activity.
- **Faith Speaks What Grace Has Provided** You speak life when you declare what God's Word says—even before you see it.
- **Words Reveal Heart Condition** If your mouth is full of doubt, your heart may be out of alignment with grace.
- **Speaking Grace Changes Atmospheres** Homes, workplaces, and even churches shift when the language of grace becomes dominant.
- **Your Confession Shapes Your Walk** The way you talk will either propel you into your calling or postpone it.

Journaling Questions

Journaling through this chapter offers the opportunity to evaluate your verbal habits and their spiritual consequences. So often we sabotage the grace we've received by speaking death instead of life, defeat instead of victory, fear instead of faith. But reflection allows you to course-correct by identifying words that no longer belong.

Let your journal be a mirror—what have you been saying in private moments? What are your default phrases when you're under pressure? As you write, let the Holy Spirit reveal not just what you've spoken—but why—and then let grace realign your confession with truth.

Speech Inventory

What kinds of words come out of my mouth when I'm tired, stressed, or frustrated? Are they grace-filled or corrupt?

_____
_____
_____

Effect on Others

Are my words building others up or tearing them down? Who has been affected by my recent speech?

_____
_____
_____
_____
_____
_____

Heart and Tongue Connection

What do my words reveal about my heart's belief in grace?

_____
_____
_____
_____
_____
_____

Faith Declaration Check

Am I regularly speaking God's Word over my life—or just rehearsing my feelings?

_____
_____
_____
_____
_____
_____

Grace-Based Goals

What changes do I need to make to ensure my speech aligns with grace?

_____
_____
_____
_____
_____
_____

Actionable Steps

Start a Speech Journal
Track your words for one day. Write down negative or doubtful phrases you say, and then rewrite them as grace-filled declarations.

Daily Grace Declarations
Each morning this week, speak three Scriptures aloud that affirm who you are in Christ and what grace has provided.

Speak to Build, Not Break
Choose one person each day this week to intentionally encourage with grace-filled words—spoken or written.

Personal Reflection

Your words carry more weight than you think. They are not background noise to your life—they are spiritual instruments. They carve the path you walk. If you want to walk in grace, you must speak in grace. Align your mouth with what God says, and watch how grace begins to flow in places where it once seemed stuck.

The good news is that no matter what you've spoken in the past, grace gives you the power to begin again. Today is a fresh invitation to align your speech with heaven and speak the language of the Kingdom—truth, love, peace, and purpose.

Am I speaking in alignment with God's grace—or against it? Do my words invite the presence of the Holy Spirit or grieve Him? Am I ready to let my confession become a carrier of grace to myself and to others?

Closing Prayer: *Father, forgive me for every word that resisted Your grace. I surrender my tongue to You today. Teach me to speak life, truth, and blessing. Let my words carry Your grace, shift atmospheres, and build faith in every place You send me. I choose to speak as one who walks in Your power. In Jesus' name, amen.*

Chapter 16

Grace to Defeat the Works of the Flesh

"Walk in the Spirit, and you shall not fulfill the lust of the flesh." (Galatians 5:16, NKJV)

There was a time in my Christian walk when I felt like I was constantly losing the battle with my flesh. I prayed, fasted, repented—yet certain patterns seemed to return like unwanted guests. I began to question whether real victory was possible, or whether I would just limp along in defeat until heaven. But everything changed the moment I stopped trying to overcome in my own strength and began to lean on the empowering force of grace. That's when the tide turned. Grace didn't just forgive me—it began to form me.

Too many believers think grace is only for forgiveness after the fact. But Scripture shows us that grace is also the power to overcome before the fall. Grace doesn't just clean you up; it holds you up. And when it comes to defeating the works of the flesh—those sinful appetites and tendencies we all battle—grace is the secret weapon. It strengthens your spirit, aligns your desires, and empowers your will.

Paul didn't say "try harder" to overcome the flesh. He said to walk in the Spirit—and that's where grace is active. The flesh craves instant satisfaction. Grace teaches long-term transformation. The flesh demands control. Grace invites surrender. The flesh works through willpower. Grace works through the Spirit. Real victory isn't about behavior modification. It's about heart transformation—and that's what grace makes possible.

So here's the truth: If you're struggling with the flesh, the answer isn't more willpower. It's more grace. The flesh has already been crucified with Christ—you just need grace to enforce the victory.

Focus Point

"Walk in the Spirit, and you shall not fulfill the lust of the flesh." (Galatians 5:16, NKJV)

This verse doesn't say "fight the flesh and you might walk in the Spirit." It says the opposite: walk in the Spirit, and the flesh will lose its grip. That's the grace path. It's not about trying harder. It's about abiding deeper. Grace doesn't empower your flesh—it empowers your spirit. And when your spirit leads, the flesh follows.

Main Theme

The heart of this chapter is the truth that grace is the divine power to overcome the works of the flesh. Victory isn't about suppressing sinful desires through effort. It's about yielding to grace, which strengthens your spirit, renews your mind, and transforms your heart. Grace is not weak—it is the strength of God made available to overcome weakness.

Grace doesn't excuse the flesh—it empowers you to overcome it.

Key Scriptures

- *"For sin shall not have dominion over you, for you are not under law but under grace." (Romans 6:14, NKJV)*
- *"And those who are Christ's have crucified the flesh with its passions and desires." (Galatians 5:24, NKJV)*
- *"Teaching us that, denying ungodliness and worldly lusts, we should live soberly, righteously, and godly in the present age." (Titus 2:12, NKJV)*

Key Points

- **Grace Is Power, Not Permission** Grace doesn't give you room to sin—it gives you strength to resist it.
- **The Flesh Is Already Defeated** The cross broke sin's power. Grace enforces that victory in your daily life.

- **Walking in the Spirit Is the Strategy** Victory comes by abiding in the Spirit—not by fighting in your flesh.
- **Grace Trains You for Godliness** Titus says grace teaches us to deny ungodliness. It's your live-in teacher, not just your pardon.
- **Legalism Strengthens the Flesh** Law provokes rebellion. Grace transforms desire.
- **Grace Changes What You Want** The more you grow in grace, the less the flesh appeals to you. Grace rewrites your appetites.
- **Victory Is a Byproduct of Abiding** When you walk with the Spirit and lean on grace, victory over the flesh is not just possible—it's promised.

Journaling Questions

Journaling through this chapter invites you to evaluate how you've been approaching your struggle with the flesh. Are you depending on your own strength—or leaning on grace? Have you seen sin as something you must suppress, or something grace can truly overcome? Reflection makes space for the Holy Spirit to reveal patterns of self-reliance and renew your understanding of grace-powered victory.

As you write, ask the Lord to show you how grace can become your new strategy—not just for survival, but for sustained transformation. Let grace train, teach, and strengthen you from the inside out.

Victory Mindset

Have I believed that real victory over the flesh is possible—or have I settled for struggle?

_____
_____
_____
_____
_____
_____
_____

Self-Reliance vs. Spirit-Walk

Am I depending on willpower to overcome sin, or am I walking in the Spirit through grace?

_____
_____
_____
_____
_____
_____

Understanding Grace's Power

Have I seen grace only as forgiveness, or do I believe it is the power to overcome temptation?

_____
_____
_____
_____
_____
_____

What Needs Crucified?

What specific work of the flesh needs to be surrendered today to grace and truth?

_____
_____
_____
_____
_____

Grace Strategy

What would it look like to practically walk in the Spirit instead of striving in the flesh this week?

_____
_____
_____
_____
_____
_____

Actionable Steps

Trade Effort for Grace
Identify one area where you've been relying on self-effort to overcome sin. Stop striving. Invite the Holy Spirit to take over. Speak out loud, "I receive grace to overcome."

Renew Your Mind with Truth
Choose a Scripture that speaks to victory over the flesh. Meditate on it daily. Let the Word wash and rewire your mindset.

Walk It Out in the Spirit
Spend 10 intentional minutes each morning in worship or prayer—just being with God. Don't ask for anything. Just walk with Him. This strengthens your spirit to lead.

Personal Reflection

The flesh doesn't define you. Grace does. Your identity is not tied to your struggle—it's rooted in your Savior. The power of sin was broken at the cross, and grace is the supply that enforces that victory daily. You don't have to live in a cycle of defeat. You have been equipped with grace to overcome.

Let this be your shift—from striving to trusting, from suppressing to surrendering, from reacting to reigning. The same grace that saved you is the grace that sanctifies you. It's time to lean into it fully.

Am I still fighting the flesh in my own strength? Have I allowed grace to take its rightful place in this battle? Am I ready to walk in the Spirit and let grace lead me to lasting victory?

Closing Prayer: *Father, thank You that the power of sin is broken and grace is greater than the flesh. I surrender my struggle today and receive the grace to walk in the Spirit. Train me, teach me, and transform me through Your grace. Let my life reflect the victory You already purchased. In Jesus' name, amen.*

Chapter 17

Empowered by Grace

"And God is able to make all grace abound toward you, that you, always having all sufficiency in all things, may have an abundance for every good work." (2 Corinthians 9:8, NKJV)

There was a moment in my life when I reached the end of my own ability. I was pouring out in ministry, handling personal challenges, and trying to keep everything afloat—but the tank was empty. I wasn't in sin. I wasn't in rebellion. I was just exhausted. And then came the whisper of the Holy Spirit, simple and clear: "You've been running in your own strength again." That's when the Lord reminded me that grace wasn't just for salvation. Grace was for power. Strength. Endurance. Overflow. Not just to get by—but to thrive.

Far too many believers think of grace only in terms of what it forgives. But Scripture teaches that grace also empowers. It is divine ability. It's not just a covering—it's a force. Grace doesn't just clean the slate—it fills your hands with supernatural capacity. When Paul faced trials, he didn't ask for more strength—he asked for more grace. And God's answer? "My grace is sufficient for you, for My strength is made perfect in weakness."

When you're empowered by grace, everything shifts. You begin to do more with less. You endure what others collapse under. You walk in peace when storms surround you. And you bear fruit—not because of talent or training—but because grace is abounding toward you. This empowerment isn't for the super spiritual—it's for anyone willing to lean in and receive.

So ask yourself today: Am I merely surviving—or am I empowered by grace for every good work? God never intended for you to limp through life. His grace is more than enough for you to run, build, serve, give, and thrive.

Focus Point

"God is able to make all grace abound toward you..." (2 Corinthians 9:8, NKJV)

This verse is a divine guarantee. It doesn't say "some grace," or "occasional grace." It says *all grace*—in *all things*—for *every good work*. God's will is not for you to be drained by your calling, but empowered in it. Grace abounds so that sufficiency becomes your new normal, and abundance becomes your new reality. Grace doesn't limit you—it equips you.

Main Theme

The central message of this chapter is that grace is the supernatural empowerment of God that enables you to do what you could never do on your own. It's not just for getting you saved—it's for getting you strong. Grace empowers you to pray with endurance, serve with joy, love with depth, and lead with confidence. If you're lacking strength, you're not lacking effort—you're likely lacking grace awareness.

Grace isn't just pardon. It's power. It's God's strength infused into your purpose.

Key Scriptures

- *"My grace is sufficient for you, for My strength is made perfect in weakness."* (2 Corinthians 12:9, NKJV)
- *"You therefore, my son, be strong in the grace that is in Christ Jesus."* (2 Timothy 2:1, NKJV)
- *"Let us have grace, by which we may serve God acceptably with reverence and godly fear."* (Hebrews 12:28, NKJV)

Key Points

- **Grace Is Divine Enablement** It's not just forgiveness—it's the fuel that empowers you to live and serve beyond your natural capacity.

- **Grace Fills the Gaps** Where your talent, strength, or knowledge ends, grace begins.
- **Weakness Is the Entry Point** Grace thrives where pride dies. Your acknowledgment of weakness invites God's strength.
- **Grace Is for Every Good Work** Whatever God calls you to do, He supplies the grace to do it—abundantly.
- **You Can Be Strong in Grace** Grace is not passive. It's something you stand in, grow in, and are strengthened by daily.
- **Empowered People Endure Well** Grace doesn't just help you start strong—it helps you finish well.
- **Grace Elevates You Beyond You** Grace doesn't make you better at being you—it makes you more like Christ.

Journaling Questions

This chapter invites you to assess whether you're truly living empowered by grace—or simply surviving through effort. Journaling helps identify the difference between natural ability and supernatural enablement. It gives the Holy Spirit room to expose where you've slipped back into self-reliance and to realign your heart with the truth that God's grace is more than enough.

As you reflect, ask the Lord to show you where grace is needed most right now. Let this be a moment of exchange—your exhaustion for His energy, your limits for His sufficiency, your striving for His strength.

Fuel Check

Am I operating in grace right now, or am I pushing through in my own strength?

_____
_____
_____
_____
_____
_____
_____

The Weakness Factor

Where do I feel weakest? Have I invited grace into that space?

_____
_____
_____
_____
_____
_____

Grace Awareness

Do I believe God's grace abounds toward me—today, right now? Why or why not?

_____
_____
_____
_____
_____
_____

Strength from Heaven

When was the last time I felt truly empowered by God? What did that look like?

_____
_____
_____
_____
_____
_____

Receiving Fresh Grace

What good work in my life right now requires me to lean harder into grace?

_____
_____
_____
_____
_____
_____

Actionable Steps

Trade Weakness for Grace
Take a specific struggle—physical, emotional, or spiritual—and verbally surrender it to God. Ask for His grace to empower you in that area today.

Strengthen Yourself in Grace
Each morning this week, declare aloud: "I am strong in the grace that is in Christ Jesus. His grace is sufficient for me."

Operate from Overflow
Choose one area of service or responsibility that's been draining you. Pause, invite grace into it, and approach it with God's empowerment instead of your effort.

Personal Reflection

You were not called to do life alone—or in your own strength. The same grace that saved you now empowers you. It carries you. It strengthens you. And it causes you to flourish even in the fire. You are not insufficient. You are not too weak. You are a candidate for grace.

Let this chapter be your turning point. You don't need more hustle. You need more grace. Step into the divine flow of empowerment. Let grace do what you cannot. Let it fuel your faith, energize your effort, and breathe life into every assignment.

Am I functioning in my own strength or in God's grace? Have I asked Him to empower my purpose today? Am I ready to exchange my weakness for His power and truly live empowered by grace?

Closing Prayer: *Father, thank You for grace that not only forgives me but empowers me. I surrender my striving and receive fresh strength from You today. Teach me to walk in grace, serve from grace, and live empowered in every good work You've called me to. Let Your sufficiency be seen in my weakness. In Jesus' name, amen.*

Harrison House is a Spirit-filled, Word of Faith Christian publisher dedicated to spreading the message of faith, hope, and love through our wide range of inspiring publications. Committed to the messages that highlight the power of the Word and Spirit, we provide books, devotionals, and study guides that empower believers to live victorious, faith-filled lives.

Our resources are designed to help readers grow spiritually, strengthen their faith, and experience the transformative power of God's Word. Harrison House is passionate about equipping Christians with the tools they need to fulfill their divine purpose and impact the world for Christ.

www.ingramcontent.com/pod-product-compliance
Lightning Source LLC
Chambersburg PA
CBHW080738230426
43665CB00020B/2779